W9-BUE-461

THE PREACHER

HIS LIFE AND WORK

YALE LECTURES

BY

J. H. JOWETT, D.D.

HARPER & BROTHERS PUBLISHERS

NEW YORK

PRINTED IN THE UNITED STATES OF AMERICA

CONTENTS

THE CALL TO BE A PREACHER

"Separated unto the Gospel of God"

L E C T U R E · O N E

THE PREACHER:
His Life and Work

THE CALL TO BE A PREACHER

"Separated unto the Gospel of God"

In the course of these lectures I am to speak on the general theme of "The Preacher: his life and work." There is little or no need of introduction. The only prefatory word I wish to offer is this. I have been in the Christian ministry for over twenty years. I love my calling. I have a glowing delight in its services. I am conscious of no distractions in the shape of any competitors for my strength and allegiance. I have had but one passion, and I have lived for it—the absorbingly arduous yet glorious work of proclaiming the grace and love of our Lord and Saviour

Jesus Christ. I stand before you, therefore, as a fellow-labourer, who has been over a certain part of the field, and my simple purpose is to dip into the pool of my experiences, to record certain practical judgments and discoveries, and to offer counsels and warnings which have been born out of my own successes and defeats.

I assume that I am speaking to men who are looking upon the field from the standpoint of the circumference, who are contemplating the work of the ministry, who are now disciplining their powers, preparing their instruments, and generally arranging their plans for a journey over what is to them a yet untravelled country. I have been over some of the roads, and I want to tell you some of the things which I have found.

I

To-day I am to speak on the Preacher's call and mission. It is of momentous importance how a man enters the ministry.

[10]

There is a " door " into this sheepfold, and there is " some other way." A man may enter as a result of merely personal calculation: or he may enter from the constraint of the purely secular counsel of his friends. He may take up the ministry as a profession, as a means of earning a living, as a desirable social distinction, as a business that offers pleasantly favourable chances of cultured leisure, of coveted leaderships, and of attractive publicity. A man may become a minister because, after carefully weighing comparative advantages, he prefers the ministry to law, or to medicine, or to science, or to trade and commerce. The ministry is ranged among many other secular alternatives, and it is chosen because of some outstanding allurement that appeals to personal taste. Now in all such decisions the candidate for the ministry misses the appointed door. His vision is entirely horizontal. His outlook is that of " the man of the world." Similar considerations are prevalent: similar maxims and axioms are assumed: the same scales of

[11]

judgment are used. The constraining motive is ambition, and the coveted goal is success. There is nothing vertical in the vision. There is no lifting up of the eyes "unto the hills." There is nothing "from above." There is no awful mysteriousness as of "a wind that bloweth where it listeth." A man has decided his calling, but "God was not in all his thoughts."

Now I hold with profound conviction that before a man selects the Christian ministry as his vocation he must have the assurance that the selection has been imperatively constrained by the eternal God. The call of the Eternal must ring through the rooms of his soul as clearly as the sound of the morning-bell rings through the valleys of Switzerland, calling the peasants to early prayer and praise. The candidate for the ministry must move like a man in secret bonds. "Necessity is laid" upon him. His choice is not a preference among alternatives. Ultimately he has no alternative: all other possibilities become dumb: there is only one clear call sounding forth

as the imperative summons of the eternal
God.

Now no man can define or describe for
another man the likeness and fashion of the
divine vocation. No man's circumstances
are exactly commensurate with another's,
and the nature of our circumstances gives
distinctiveness and originality to our call.
Moreover the Lord honours our individuality in the very uniqueness of the call
He addresses to us. The singularity of our
circumstances, and the awful singularity
of our souls, provide the medium through
which we hear the voice of the Lord. How
strangely varied are the " settings " through
which the divine voice determines the vocations of men, as they are recorded in the
Scriptures! Here is Amos, a poor herdman, brooding deeply and solitarily amid
the thin pastures of Tekoa. And rumours
come his way of dark doings in the high
places of the land. Wealth is breeding
prodigality. Luxury is breeding callous-
ness. Injustice is rampant, and " truth is
fallen in the streets." And as the poor

herdman mused " the fire burned." On
those lone wastes he heard a mysterious
call and he saw a beckoning hand! For
him there was no alternative road. "The
Lord took me as I followed the flock, and
said, Go, prophesy!"

But how different is the setting in the
call of the Prophet Isaiah! Isaiah was a
friend of kings: he was a cultured fre-
quenter of courtly circles: he was at home
in the precincts of kings' courts. And
through what medium did the divine call
sound to this man? " In the year that
King Uzziah died I saw the Lord." Isaiah
had pinned his faith to Uzziah. Uzziah was
" the pillar of a people's hopes." Upon
his strong and enlightened sovereignty was
being built a purified and stable state.
And now the pillar had fallen, and it
seemed as though all the fair and promising structure would topple with it, and
the nation would drop again into unclean-
ness and confusion. But on the empty
throne Isaiah discovered the presence of
God. A human pillar had crumbled: the

Pillar of the universe remained. " In the year that King Uzziah died I saw the Lord." Isaiah had a vision of a mighty God, with a vaster sovereignty, moving and removing men as the ministers of His large and beneficent purpose. Isaiah mourned the fall of a king, and he heard a call to service! " Whom shall I send, and who will go for me? " One man fallen: another man wanted! God's call sounded through the impoverished ranks, and smote the heart and conscience of Isaiah, and Isaiah found his vocation and his destiny. " Here am I, send me! "

How different, again, are the circumstances attending the call of Jeremiah! There are liquids which a " shake " will precipitate into solids: and there are fluid and nebulous things in life, vague things lying back in the mists of consciousness, which some sudden shaking or shifting of circumstances can precipitate into clear intuition, into firm knowledge, and we have the mind and will of God. Yes, a little tilt of circumstances, and the mist becomes a vision, and uncertainty changes into realized destiny. I think it was even so with Jeremiah. In his life there had been thinkings without conclusions, obscure moments of consciousness without clear guidance, broodings without definite vocations. But one day, we know not how, his circumstances slightly shifted, and his vague meditation changed into vivid conviction, and he heard the voice of the Lord God saying unto him, " Before thou camest forth out of the womb I sanctified thee, and I ordained thee a prophet." It was a clear call: like lightning rather than light: and it was greatly feared, and reluctantly accepted.

I have given three examples of the varying fashions in the callings of our God: but had they been indefinitely multiplied, until they had included the last one in my audience to hear the mystic voice, it would be found that every genuine call has its own uniqueness, and that through the originality of personal circumstances the divine call is mediated to the individual soul. And

so we cannot tell how the call will come
to us, what will be the manner of its coming. It may be that the divine constraint
will be as soft and gentle as a glance: " I
will guide thee with Mine eye." It may
be that we can scarcely describe the guidance, it is so shy, and quiet, and unobtrusive. Or it may be that the constraint
will seize us as with a strong and invisible
grip, as though we were in the custody of
an iron hand from which we cannot escape.
That, I think, is the significance of the
strangely violent figure used by the Prophet
Isaiah: " The Lord said unto me *with a
strong hand."* The divine calling laid hold
of the young prophet as though with a
" strong hand " that imprisoned him like
a vice! He felt he had no alternative! He
was carried along by divine coercion!
" Necessity was laid " upon him! He was
" in bonds " and he must obey. And I
think this feeling of the " strong hand,"
this sense of mysterious coercion, is sometimes a dumb constraint which offers but
little illumination to the judgment. What

I mean is this: a man may realize his call to the ministry in the powerful imperative of a dumb grip for which he can offer no adequate reason. He is sure of the constraint. It is as manifest as gravity. But when he seeks for explanations to justify himself he feels he is moving in the twilight or in the deeper mystery of the night. He knows the " feel " of the " strong hand " that moves him, but he cannot give a satisfactory interpretation of the movement. If I may say it without needless obtrusion, this was the character of my own earliest call into the ministry. For a time I was like a blind man who is being led by the " strong hand " of a silent guide. There was the guidance of a mysterious coercion, but there was no open vision. I was " in bonds," but I knew the " hand," and I had to obey. " I will bring the blind by a way that they knew not." " Thou hast laid Thine hand upon me."

And so it is that the manner of one man's " call " may be very different to the manner of another man's " call," but in the essential matter they are one and the same. I would affirm my own conviction that in all genuine callings to the ministry there is a sense of the divine initiative, a solemn communication of the divine will, a mysterious feeling of commission, which leaves a man no alternative, but which sets him in the road of this vocation bearing the ambassage of a servant and instrument of the eternal God. " For whosoever shall call upon the name of the Lord shall be saved. How then shall they call on Him in whom they have not believed? and how shall they believe on Him of whom they have not heard? and how shall they hear without a preacher? and how shall they preach *except they be sent?* " The assurance of being sent is the vital part of our commission. But hear again the word of God: " I have not sent these prophets, yet they ran: I have not spoken to them, yet they prophesied." The absence of the sense of vocation will eviscerate a man's responsibility, and will tend to secularize his ministry from end to end.

[19]

Now a man who enters through the door of divine vocation into the ministry will surely apprehend " the glory " of his calling. He will be constantly wondering, and his wonder will be a moral antiseptic, that *he* has been appointed a servant in the treasuries of grace, to make known " the unsearchable riches of Christ." You cannot get away from that wonder in the life of the Apostle Paul. Next to the infinite love of his Saviour, and the amazing glory of his own salvation, his wonder is arrested and nourished by the surpassing glory of his own vocation. His " calling " is never lost in the medley of professions. The light of privilege is always shining on the way of duty. His work never loses its halo, and his road never becomes entirely commonplace and grey. He seems to catch his breath every time he thinks of his mission, and in the midst of abounding adversity glory still more abounds. And, therefore, this is the sort of music and song that we find unceasing, from the hour of his conversion and calling to the hour of his death:

"Unto me, who am less than the least of all saints, is this grace given, that I should preach among the Gentiles the unsearchable riches of Christ." "For this cause I Paul, the prisoner of Jesus Christ for you Gentiles, if ye have heard of the dispensation of the grace of God which is given me to you-ward!" "Whereunto I am ordained a preacher, and an apostle, a teacher of the Gentiles in faith and verity!" Do you not feel a sacred, burning wonder in these exclamations, a holy, exulting pride in his vocation, leagued with a marvelling humility that the mystic hand of ordination had rested upon him? That abiding wonder was part of his apostolic equipment, and his sense of the glory of his calling enriched his proclamation of the glories of redeeming grace. If we lose the sense of the wonder of our commission we shall become like common traders in a common market, babbling about common wares.

I think you will find that all great preachers have preserved this wondering sense of the greatness of their vocation.

It was most impressively true of Dr. Dale, a distinguished Yale lecturer, and my illustrious predecessor in the pulpit at Carrs Lane. The members of my old congregation have often tried to describe to me the mingled dignity and humility with which he proclaimed the gospel of salvation. They say that at times he spake with a sort of personal diffidence born of a great surprise that he should be counted worthy to " bear the vessels of the Lord." They tell me that it was peculiarly manifest at the table of the Lord, and at other times, when, in the handling of the most august themes, he was leading his people into the innermost secrets of the holy place. All this was equally true of another man, very different in mental equipment to Dr. Dale, Robert M'Cheyne, who, in Scotland, brought the riches of grace to an almost countless multitude. Andrew Bonar, M'Cheyne's intimate friend, has told us with what full and delicate wonder he carried his ministry in the Lord. In their conversation he would frequently break out into deep and joyful surprise. The glory of his ministry irradiated common duty like a halo, and God's statutes became his songs. I do not marvel that Andrew Bonar can write these words about him: " He was so reverent toward God, so full also in desire toward Him . . . he never seemed unprepared. His lamp was always burning, and his loins always girt. His forgetfulness of all that was not found to God's glory was remarkable, and there seemed never a time when he was not himself feeling the presence of God."

This sense of great personal surprise in the glory of our vocation, while it will keep us humble, will also make us great. It will save us from becoming small officials in transient enterprises. It will make us truly big, and will, therefore, save us from spending our days in trifling. Emerson has somewhere said that men whose duties are done beneath lofty and stately domes acquire a dignified stride and a certain stateliness of demeanour. And preachers of the gospel, whose work is done beneath the

lofty dome of some glorious and wonderful
conception of their ministry, will acquire
a certain largeness of demeanour in which
flippancy and trivialities cannot breathe.
" I shall run the way of Thy commandments *when Thou shalt enlarge my heart."*

Now, if such be the sacredness of our
calling, and its consequent glory, we cannot
be blind to its solemn responsibilities. It is
a great, awful, holy trust. We are called
to be guides and guardians of the souls
of men, leading them into " the way of
peace." We are to be constantly engaged
with eternal interests, leading the thoughts
and wills of men to the things that pri-
marily matter, and disengaging them from
lesser or meaner concerns which hold them
in servitude. We are to be the friends of
the Bridegroom, winning men, not to ourselves, but to Him, match-making for the
Lord, abundantly satisfied when we have
brought the bride and the Bridegroom together. I do not wonder that men shrink
from the calling even when they feel the
glory of it! I do not wonder at the holy

fear of men as they approach the sacred
office! Listen to these words of Charles
Kingsley, written in his private journal,
written in the dawning of the day on
which he was to be ordained to the priest-
hood of the Lord: " In a few hours my
whole soul will be waiting silently for the
seals of admission to God's service, of which
honour I dare hardly think myself worthy
. . . Night and morning for months my
prayer has been, Oh, God, if I am not
worthy, if my sin in leading souls away
from Thee is still unpardoned, if I am
desiring to be a deacon not wholly for
the sake of serving Thee, if it is necessary
to show me my weakness and the holiness
of Thy office still more strongly, Oh, God,
reject me!" I say I do not wonder at
the shrinking, and I would not pray that
the day may come when it may entirely
pass away, lest in a perilous self-confidence
we lose the brightness of the glory, and
have an impoverished conception of our
great vocation. In this matter, as in many
others, " the fear of the Lord is a fountain

of life," and " the fear of the Lord is the
beginning of wisdom."

II

Such, then, is the preacher's calling, so
sacred, so responsible, so glorious; what
can be the mission of such a vocation?
Have we any clear word of enlightenment
which places it before us like a shining
road? I think we have. Whenever I want
to recover afresh the superlatively lofty
mission of my calling I reverently turn
into the holy place where our Master is in
communion with the Father, and in that
mysterious fellowship I hear my calling
defined. " As Thou hast sent Me into the
world, even so have I also sent them into
the world." The serenity that pervades
that sequence is overwhelming. The
quietude of the passage is the quietude of
stupendous heights. It is the serenity of
sublimity. The " even so " which asso-
ciates the two sentences on the same level
of thought and purpose is majestic and
divine. It places the mission of the Gali-

lean fishermen in line with the redemptive
mission of the Son of God.

Let us move reverently in that secret
holy place. " As Thou hast sent Me." The
words lead our halting, failing thought into
the inconceivable state which our Lord
described as " The glory which I had with
Thee before the world was." I know that
we have neither wing with which to soar
into the mysterious realm nor eye where-
with to see the burning bliss. But we
may feel the majesty of what we cannot
express. It is well to feel the awe of the
undefined and the indefinable. And it is
well to lose ourselves in the vast significance
of words like these, " The glory which I
had with Thee before the world was."
Brood upon it. The sublime abode! The
holy Fatherhood! The light ineffable! The
mystic presences! The cherubim and seraphim who " continually do cry, Holy, Holy,
Holy!" And then in that glory the
redemptive mission of the Prince of Glory!
A wonder more glorious than the glory is
the laying of the glory by! " He emptied

[27]

Himself." The amazement of the spirits that surround the throne! "The word became flesh." The wonder of it! The awe of it! "As Thou hast sent Me into the world."

And now change the scene. The inconceivable glory is laid aside. The Son of Glory is no longer surrounded by cherubim and seraphim, swift and pure as light. But in the guise of a Galilean peasant He has a few fishermen around Him, dull in apprehension of spiritual purpose, timid in heart, irresolute in will, often seeking personal advancement rather than the progress of truth, very lame, very dense, altogether very imperfect and soon to forsake Him and flee.

And these two scenes are linked together. "As Thou hast sent Me into the world, even so have I also sent them into the world." That the one "going out" should be linked with the other is to me the wonder of wonders. The marvel is that they should be mentioned in the same breath, included in the same bundle of thought, comprehended in the same purpose. For what does the association mean? It means the exaltation of Christian apostleship, the glorification of the Christian ministry. It means that the mystic ordination that rested on the Son of Glory, when He came to earth, rested also on the fisherman Peter as he went down to Cæsarea. It means that the same holy commission that wrought in the redemptive ministry of the Son of God wrought also in the energies of the Apostle Paul as he went forth to Macedonia, and on to Corinth, and Athens, and Rome. It means that you, in your sphere of service, and I in mine, may, in our own degree, share the same joyous commission as was held by the Prince of Glory when He was made in the likeness of man. It is the glorification of the apostle's mission and service. " As Thou hast sent Me."

We must, therefore, look carefully at what is said about the nature and character of our Lord's mission if we would understand our own commission, and so realize the glory of our own appointment and the dignity of our own service. We must reverently gaze upon the one that we may thereby apprehend the other. Have we any further guidance concerning the mission of our Lord? Did He define it? Did He describe it? Has He anywhere outlined it in features that we can comprehend? I think such light has been given us. We are told that Jesus went into Nazareth on the Sabbath day. He entered the synagogue. He opened a book and read a selected passage, and then He appropriated the words as descriptive of Himself, and as finding fulfilment in His own life. And what was the passage? " He hath sent Me to preach the gospel to the poor, to heal the broken-hearted, to preach deliverance to the captives, and recovering of sight to the blind; to set at liberty them that are bruised and to proclaim the acceptable year of the Lord." Is it possible that the passage is a lamp whereby we may interpret our own ministry? Look at the cardinal words in the passage, " preach," " heal," " deliver," " give liberty," " proclaim " ! Can we extract the common virtue of the words? Have they any general significance? Is there any common denominator? May we not say that in all these varied words there is a pervasive sentiment and purpose of emancipation? Are they not all suggestive of an opening, an emergence, a release? Let us review the words: " Sent to preach "; to give the open vision of divine grace to those whose thought is darkly bounded and imprisoned. " To heal "; to give the grace of comfort to those who are crushed beneath the unintelligible weight of sorrow and care. " To deliver the captive "; to give the open spaces of a noble freedom to all who languish in any form of unholy servitude. " To set at liberty them that are bruised "; to give open passage to all who are lying with broken wing or broken limb, to all whose powers have been shattered by disappointment and defeat. " To proclaim the acceptable year of the Lord "; to announce

the open door in the present hour, and to
say that by God's grace there is a present
right of way from the deepest gloom of the
soul into the radiant light of acceptance
with God. In all these words there appears to be this general sense of emergence
and release. There is an opening of mind,
an opening of heart, an opening of eyes, an
opening of doors. In every word the iron
gate swings back and there is the sound of
the song of freedom.

Now in the light of these words dare
we take up the Master's sequence and give
this same interpretation to our own mission and service? I think this is our holy
privilege. It is one aspect of " The prize
of the high calling of God in Christ
Jesus." " As Thou hast sent Me into the
world even so have I also sent them,"—to
preach, to heal, to deliver, to open the iron
gates, to be the ambassadors of a glorious
freedom for body, mind, and soul. Yes, I
think we may accept this interpreting light
upon our calling; the mission of the apostle
is determined by the mission of the Master,

and that mission is declared to be one of wide and inclusive emancipation.

If this be so, if we may read our calling in the words of the Master, by what method are we to follow the ministry of emancipation? We are to follow it in two ways, by the service of good news, and by the good news of service. First, we are to find our mission in the service of good news. That is our primary calling, to be tellers of good news, to be heralds of salvation. Here are the emphatic words: "Preach!" and again, "Preach!" "Proclaim!" "As ye go, preach!" And what is to be the theme of the good news? This we will consider in greater detail later on. But meanwhile let this be said. It is to be good news about God. It is to be good news about the Son of God. It is to be good news about the vanquishing of guilt and the forgiveness of sins. It is to be good news about the subjection of the world and the flesh and the devil. It is to be good news about the transfiguration of sorrow and the withering of a thousand

[33]

bitter roots of anxiety and care. It is to be good news about the stingless death and the spoiled and beaten grave. That is to be our first mission to the world,—to be carriers of good news. That is to be our glorious mission. We are to go about our ways finding men and women shattered and broken, with care upon them, and sorrow upon them, and death upon them, wrinkled in body and mind, and with the light flickering out in their souls. And we are to bring them the news which will be like oil to dying lamps, which will be as vitalizing air to those who faint, which will be like the power of new wing to birds that have been broken in flight. " The words that I speak unto you, they are spirit and they are life."

But we are not only to preach the good news. We are also to incarnate it in vital service. Our mission is to be one of emancipation both by word and work, by gospel and by crusade. Everywhere we are confronted by big iniquities, frowning like embattled castles. Around us are grim prisons where innocence lies entombed. All over the world captives are held in a thousand evil servitudes. And here is our mission, which is reflected from the mission of our Lord, " He hath sent me to give liberty to the captives." The word of grace is to be confirmed by gracious deeds. The Gospel is to be corroborated by the witness of daring exploits. The herald is to be a knight, revealing the power of his message in his own chivalry. That is to say, there is laid upon the preacher the supreme privilege of obligation and sacrifice. He is to be filled with the " love and pity " which are the very energies of redemption. The good news without the good deed will leave us impotent. But the spirit of sacrificial love will make us invincible.

There is much that might make us afraid. The very terms of our commission might fill us with dread. " I send you forth as sheep in the midst of wolves." How quixotic the enterprise appears to be! Let our thoughts go back to the first preaching crusaders, so apparently weak and fearless as to be compared to innocent sheep! And these men are sent forth into a wolfish environment, where the odds appear to be overwhelming, and the outlook one of hopeless and cruel defeat. And the words of the commission are unchanged. Still does the Master say to you and me, " I send you forth as sheep in the midst of wolves,"—against cruelty, and lust, and greed, and indifference, against every form of sin, against an army of antagonists, fierce and terrific. What is to be our inspiration and our confidence? I will dare to place two separated passages side by side that I may offer you the heartening secret of their communion. And here is one of them: " As Thou hast sent Me into the world." And here is the other: " Behold the Lamb! " The Lord who was sent into the brutal or indifferent environment of man was the Lamb of God! The Lamb came among wolves. And now let me place another pair of passages side by side, and the analogy will help us forward to the inspiration we need. And here is one: " Even so have I also sent them into the world." And here is the other: " I send you forth as sheep." The Lamb of God Himself came among the wolves. And He sends His sheep among the same fierce and destructive presences. The Lamb sends forth the sheep!

And how fared it with the Lamb? I turn to the Word of God and I read: " These shall make war with the Lamb and the Lamb shall overcome." And I read again: " And I beheld, and in the midst of the throne stood the Lamb." The Lamb was triumphant. It was not the wolf who conquered, but the Lamb, and in the victory of the Lamb the safety and triumph of the sheep are assured. That is our inspiration. " In the world ye shall have tribulation, but be of good cheer, I have overcome the world." We are " called with a holy calling." Our mission is beset with antagonisms. The way will rarely, if ever, be easy. But in chivalrous faith and obedience our victory is secure.

THE PERILS OF THE PREACHER

"Lest . . . I myself should be a castaway"

LECTURE . TWO

THE PERILS OF THE PREACHER

"Lest . . . I myself should be a cast-away"

I BEGIN our consideration of the perils of the preacher by quoting this startling word of the Apostle Paul. "I therefore so run, not as uncertainly: so fight I, not as one that beateth the air; but I keep under my body, and bring it into subjection: lest that by any means, when I have preached to others, I myself should be a castaway." And, as you well know, the word which is here translated "cast-away," and in the Revised Version is translated "rejected," is applied to things that cannot bear the standard test, that reveal themselves to be counterfeit and worthless, like coins which have no true "ring" about them, and which are flung aside as spurious and base. And the Apostle Paul foresees the possible peril of his becoming a counterfeit coin in the sacred currency, a spurious dealer in sublime realities, a worthless guide to "the unsearchable riches of Christ." He sees the insurgent danger of men who are busy among holy things becoming profane. A man may be dealing with "gold thrice refined," and yet he himself may be increasingly mingled with the dross of the world. He may lead others into the heavenly way and he may lose the road himself. He may be diligent in his holy calling and yet be deepeningly degenerate. It is the ominous forecast of what is perhaps life's saddest and most pathetic tragedy, the spectacle of a man who, having "preached to others," should himself become "a castaway."

Now the Apostle Paul foresaw the peril, and studiously and prayerfully provided against it. And you and I have been chosen to walk along his road, and we shall encounter all the dangers that infest it. None of us will be immune from their besetment. Perils are ever the attendants of privilege, and they are thickest round about the most exalted stations. I suppose that

every profession and every trade has its
own peculiar enemies, just as every kind
of flower is attacked by its own peculiar
pests. And I suppose that every profession might claim that these distinctive mi-
crobes are most subtle and plentiful in its
own particular sphere of service. And yet
I strongly believe that the artisan who
works with his hands, or the trader who is
busy in commerce, or the professional man
who labours in law, or in medicine, or in
literature, or in music, or art, is not able
to conceive the insidious and deadly perils
which infest the life of a minister. The
pulpit is commonly regarded as a charmed
circle, where " the destruction that wasteth
at noonday " never arrives. We are looked
upon as the children of favour, " delicately
apparelled," shielded in many ways from
the cutting blasts that sweep across the
common life. It is supposed there is many
a bewitching temptation that never dis-
plays its shining wares at our window!
There is many a gnawing care that never
shows its teeth at our gate! We are told

[43]

we have the genial times, and the "soft raiment," and that for us life is more a garden than a battlefield.

But, gentlemen, the fatal defect in the statement is this:—it reasons as though "privilege" spells "protection," and as though soft conditions provide immunity. It reasons as though a garden is a fortress, and as though a favoured life is a strong defence. It reasons as though a garden can never be a battlefield, when after all a garden was the scene of the hardest fighting in the battle of Waterloo. Privilege never confers security: it rather provides the conditions of the fiercest strife. I gladly and gratefully recognize that the minister is laden with many privileges, but I also recognize that the measure of our privileges is just the measure of our dangers, that the inventory of our garden would also give an inventory of the destructive pests that haunt every flower, and shrub, and tree. It is literally and awfully true that "where grace abounds" death also may abound, for our spiritual favours

may be either " a savour of life unto life
or of death unto death." We may lead
people into wealth and we ourselves may be
counterfeit: we may preach to others while
we ourselves are castaways. I propose,
therefore, to examine some of these perils
which fatten upon privilege, these enemies
which will haunt you to the very end of
your ministerial life.

The first peril which I will name, and I
name it first because its touch is so fatal,
is that of *deadening familiarity with the
sublime.* You will not have been long in
the ministry before you discover that it is
possible to be fussily busy about the Holy
Place and yet to lose the wondering sense
of the Holy Lord. We may have much to
do with religion and yet not be religious.
We may become mere guide-posts when we
were intended to be guides. We may indicate the way, and yet not be found in it.
We may be professors but not pilgrims.
Our studies may be workshops instead of
" upper rooms." Our share in the table-
provisions may be that of analysts rather

than guests. We may become so absorbed in words that we forget to eat the Word. And the consummation of the subtle peril may be this: we may come to assume that fine talk is fine living, that expository skill is deep piety, and while we are fondly hugging the non-essentials the veritable essence escapes.

I think this is one of the most insidious, and perhaps the predominant peril in a preacher's life. A man may live in mountain-country and lose all sense of the heights. And that is a terrible impoverishment, when mountain-country comes to have the ordinary significance of the plains. The preacher is called upon to dwell among the stupendous concerns of human interest. The mountainous aspects of life are his familiar environment. He lives almost every hour in sight of the immensities and the eternities—the awful sovereignty of God, and the glorious yet cloud-capped mysteries of redeeming grace. But here is the possible tragedy: he may live in constant sight of these tremendous presences and may cease to see them. They may come to be mere "lay-figures" of the study, no longer the appalling dignities which prostrate the soul in adoration and awe. That is our peril. We have to be constantly talking about these things, and the talking may be briskly continued even when the things themselves have been lost. We may retain our interest in philosophy, and lose our reverence. We may keep up a busy traffic in words, but "the awe of the heights" no longer makes us tremble with urgent actuality. We may talk about the mountains, and we may do it as blind insensitive children of the plains. The plentifulness of our privileges may make us numb. "Will a man leave the snow of Lebanon?" The calamity is that we may do so and never know it.

The second peril in the preacher's life which I will name is that of *deadening familiarity with the commonplace.* I have mentioned the possibility of our becoming callous to the presence of the heights: there is an equally subtle peril of our becoming dead to the bleeding tragedies of common life. Dark presences which come to others only as occasional and startling visitors are in our fellowship every day. They move in our daily surroundings. Experiences which move and arrest the business-man, because they are unusual, are the ordinary furniture of our lives. And the ever possible danger is this, that in becoming accustomed to tragedy we may also become callous.

There is, for example, our familiarity with death. I know there is something about Death so mysterious, so imperious, that he never passes as quite an ordinary presence. The chill air of his passing is never altogether lost. And yet you will find it is possible to be strangely unmoved in the house of death. There will be breaking hearts around you, among whom Death has come like some cruel beast, heedlessly breaking and crushing the fragile reeds on his way to the water-courses, and they are feeling that they will never be able to lift themselves again into the sweet sunny

light and air. And you may be like an indifferent outsider in the tragedy! I know
that it may be one of God's merciful dealings with us, as a necessity of our labour,
to put the gracious cushion of custom between us and the immediate blows of dark
and heavy circumstance. No man could
do his work if the vital drain were to be
unrelieved. If custom gave us no defence
we should faint from sheer exhaustion.
The impact of the blow upon us is re-
strained in order that we may minister to
those upon whom it has fallen with naked
and staggering force. But that possible
ministry becomes impossible if the cushion
becomes a stone. If familiarity implies
insensibility then our powers of consolation
are lost.

Now this is one of our perils, and it is
very real and immediate. The peril can be
avoided, but there it is, one of the possible
dangers in your way. Familiarity may be
deadly, and we may be as dead men in
the usually disturbing presences of sorrow,
and pain, and death. The pathetic may

cease to melt us, the tragic may cease to shock us. We may lose our power to weep. The very fountain of our tears may be dried up. The visitations which arouse and vivify our fellowmen may put us into a fatal sleep. A stupor begotten of familiarity may make us remote from the common need. To use the apostle's phrase, we may become " past feeling."

The third ministerial peril is *the possible perversion of our emotional life.* The preaching of the gospel of the Lord Jesus Christ demands and creates in the preacher a certain power of worthy emotion, and this very emotion becomes the centre of new ministerial danger. For the emotions can become perverted. They may become unhealthily intense and inflammatory. They may become defiled. The emotional may so easily become the neurotic. I do not know just how to express the danger I see. A preacher's emotion may be so constantly and so profoundly wrought upon that his moral defences are imperilled. Exaggerated emotion can be like a flood that will overwhelm and submerge his moral dykes, and plunge him into irretrievable disaster.

I remember one very eventful day when I had a long walk with Hugh Price Hughes through the city of London. In the course of our conversation he suddenly stopped, and gripping my arm in his impulsive way, he said, " Jowett, the evangelical preacher is always on the brink of the abyss! " There may be excessive colouring in the judgment, but it indicates a grave peril which it is imperative to name, and against which we should be on our guard. I think I know what he meant. Preaching that sways the preacher's emotions, moving him like a gale upon the sea, makes great demands upon the nerves, and sometimes produces nervous exhaustion. That is to say, the evangelical preacher, with his constant business in great facts and verities that sway the feelings, may become the victim of nervous depression, and in his nervous impoverishment his moral defences may be relaxed, the enemy may leap within his gates, and his spirit may be imprisoned in dark and carnal bondage. " He that hath ears to hear let him hear," and " let him that thinketh he standeth take heed lest he fall."

And now let me mention a peril which will be more evident than the one I have just named, because we meet it along every road of life, and because we make its acquaintance long before we take up the actual work of the ministry. I mean *the perilous gravitation of the world*. I say you may meet that danger everywhere, but nowhere will you meet it in a more insidious and persistent fashion than in the Christian ministry. It is round about us like a malaria, and we may become susceptible to its contagion. It offers itself as a climate, and we may be led into accepting it as the atmosphere of our lives. I suppose that one of the deepest characteristics of worldliness is an illicit spirit of compromise. It calls itself by many agreeable names, such as " expediency," " tactfulness," " diplomacy," and it sometimes ascends to higher rank and claims kinship with " geniality," " sociability," and " friendship." But, despite this fine borrowed attire, the worldly spirit of compromise is just the sacrifice of the moral ideal to the popular standard, and the subjection of personal conviction to current opinion. There is a half-cynical counsel given in the Book of Ecclesiastes which exactly describes what I am seeking to express. " Be not righteous overmuch. . . . Be not overmuch wicked." I think this moral advice enshrines the very genius of worldliness. Worldly compromise takes the medium-line between white and black, and wears an ambiguous grey. It is a partisan of neither midnight nor noon. It prefers the twilight, which is just a mixture of midnight and noon and is equally related to both. It is, therefore, a very specious presence, fraternizing with all sorts and conditions of men, nodding acquaintedly to the saint, and intimately recognizing the sinner, at home everywhere, mixing with the worshippers in the temple, or with the money-changers in the temple courts. Grey is a very useful colour, it is in keeping with a wedding or a funeral. And yet the word of Holy Writ is clear and decisive, raising the most exalted standard: "Keep thy garments always white."

Now you will meet that spirit of worldly compromise, and you will meet it in its most seductive form. It will seek to determine the character of your personal life. It will entice you to wear grey habits when you mix with the business-men of your congregation, and to " talk grey " in your conversation with them. A certain suavity or urbanity will offer itself as a medium, and you will loll about with relaxed moral ideals. This is no idle fancy. I am describing the road along which many a minister has passed to deadly degeneracy and impotence. We are tempted to leave our " noontide lights " behind in our study, and to move among men of the world with a dark lantern which we can manipulate to suit our company. We pay the tribute of smiles to the low business standard. We

pay the tribute of laughter to the fashion-
able jest. We pay the tribute of easy
tolerance to ambiguous pleasures. We
soften everything to a comfortable acquies-
cence. We seek to be " all things to all
men " to please all. We " run with the
hare " and we " hunt with the hounds."
We try to " serve God and mammon."
We become the victims of illicit compromise. There is nothing distinctive about
our character. It is neither one thing nor
another. We are of the kind described by
the Prophet Isaiah: " Thy wine is mixed
with water," or like those portrayed by
Jeremiah: " Reprobate silver shall men
call thee."

But in the perilous gravitation of worldliness there is more than an illicit spirit of
compromise: there is what I will call the
fascination of the glittering. All through
our ministry we are exposed to the tempta-
tions which met our Lord in the wilderness, and which met Him again and again
before He reached the cross. " All these
things will I give Thee if Thou wilt fall

down and worship me." It was the presentation of carnal splendour, the offer of an immediate prize. The tempter used the lure of the "showy," and he sought to eclipse the vision of reality. He used the glittering to entice the eyes away from the "gold thrice refined."

That peril will meet you on the very day your ministry begins. Nay, it is with you now in the days of preparation. Even now you may be arrested by fireworks and you may lose the vision of the stars. On your ordination day you may be the victim of worldliness, and your soul may be prostrate before Mammon. You may be seeking "the Kingdoms of the world and the glory of them"; in quest of "glitter" rather than true "gold." We are tempted to covet a showy eloquence rather than the deep, unobtrusive "spirit of power." We may become more intent on full pews than on redeemed souls. We may be more concerned to have a swelling membership-roll than to have the names of our people "written in Heaven." We may be more keen for "the praises of men" than for "the good pleasure of God." These are the perils of worldliness. Our besetting peril is to go after the "showy," to "strive," and "cry," to let our voice be heard "in the streets," to follow the glitter instead of "the gleam," and to be satisfied if our names are sounded pleasantly in the crumbling halls of worldly fame.

I have thus mentioned many perils which will meet you in your calling, and they have this common and fatal tendency, to snare you away from God. They will lead you away from "the snows of Lebanon." from the great gathering-ground of your resources, where the mighty rivers rise which bring to men the dynamic of a strong and efficient ministry. And, surely, of all pathetic sights on God's earth there is none more pathetic than a preacher of the gospel who, by the benumbing power of custom, or by the wiles and guiles of the world, has been separated from his God! For when a preacher, by an unhal-

lowed absorption in the mere letter of truth,
or by a successful invasion of worldliness,
gets away from God, the direful conse-
quences are immediate and destructive.
Let me mention some of the results.

First of all, our characters will lose their
spirituality. We shall lack that fine fragrance which makes people know that we
dwell in " the King's gardens." There will
be no " heavenly air " about our spirits.
Atmospheres will not be mysteriously
changed by our presence. We shall no
longer bring the strength of mountain-air
into close and fusty fellowships. And,
surely, this ought to be one of the most
gracious services of a Christian minister,—
by his very presence to create a climate by
which the faint and overburdened are re-
vived. There is an exquisite line in Paul's
portrayal of his friend Onesiphorus which
describes this very characteristic of ministerial service. " He oft refreshed me," and
the refreshment is just the bringing of
fresh air, a vitalizing breath, a restoring
climate for faint and weary souls! The

coming of Onesiphorus was like the opening of a window to one held in close imprisonment. He brought an atmosphere
with him, and he himself had found it in
the breathing of the Holy Ghost. My
brethren, it is our spirituality that provides that atmosphere of refreshment, and
it is active in our silences as well as in
our speech. If we are snared away from
God that atmosphere is devitalized, our
personal " air " loses its power of quickening, and no " faint-heart " calls down blessings as we pass by.

But a second thing happens when, for
any cause, we are separated from the Lord
whom we have vowed to serve. Our speech
lacks a mysterious impressiveness. We
are wordy but we are not mighty. We
are eloquent but we do not persuade.
We are reasonable but we do not convince.
We preach much but we accomplish little. We teach but we do not woo. We
make a " show of power " but men do not
move. Men come and go, they may be
interested or amused, but they do not bow

[59]

in penitent surrender at the feet of the
Lord. We go on talking, talking, talking, and the haunts of " the evil one " ring
with scorn of our futility. Our words are
just the " enticing words of man's wisdom," they are not " in demonstration of
the Spirit and of power."

And as it is with our preaching so it is
with our enterprises. If our perils overwhelm us our enterprises become pastimes
rather than crusades. We are busy but we
are futile. We may be always active but
the strongholds do not fall. We pass multitudes of resolutions but nobody quakes.
We form clubs and societies but there is
no vital movement towards God. The
central fact of the matter is this: when a
preacher is snared away from God and
from the good-pleasure of God he does
not count, and he is, therefore, not counted,
and evil dances flippantly along the open
road heedless of his presence, because he
has no magic weapon by which it can be
either crippled or destroyed.

But I turn to a more positive aspect

of my theme. How can all these perils be avoided? Nay, how can we make our perils minister to a richer, stronger, and more fruitful life? For that is life's true victory, not to ignore dangers but to despoil them. It is possible to take the strength of a peril and enlist it in our own resources. That is the privilege of temptation: we can sack it and transfer the wealth of its strength into the treasury of our own will. That is a great principle! The minister's life has many perils, and he has, therefore, many possible stores of enrichment. We cannot affirm this to ourselves too often and too confidently: conquered perils become allies: in every victory there is a transfer of dynamics. Perils may indicate our possible impoverishment: they equally indicate our possible enrichment.

How, then, is it to be done? By studious and reverent regard to the supreme commonplaces of the spiritual life. We must assiduously attend to the culture of our souls. We must sternly and systematically make time for prayer, and

for the devotional reading of the Word
of God. We must appoint private seasons
for the deliberate and personal appropria-
tion of the Divine Word, for self-examina-
tion in the presence of its warnings, for
self-humbling in the presence of its judgments, for self-heartening in the presence
of its promises, and for self-invigoration
in the presence of its glorious hopes. In
the midst of our fussy, restless activities,
in all the multitudinous trifles which, like
a cloud of dust, threaten to choke our souls,
the minister must fence off his quiet and
secluded hours, and suffer no interference
or obtrusion. I offer that counsel with
particular urgency now that I have come
to labour in this country. I am profoundly
convinced that one of the gravest perils
which beset the ministry of this country
is a restless scattering of energies over an
amazing multiplicity of interests, which
leaves no margin of time or of strength for
receptive and absorbing communion with
God. We are tempted to be always " on
the run," and to measure our fruitfulness

[62]

by our pace and by the ground we cover in the course of the week!

Gentlemen, we are not always doing the most business when we seem to be most busy. We may think we are truly busy when we are really only restless, and a little studied retirement would greatly enrich our returns. We are great only as we are God-possessed; and scrupulous appointments in the upper room with the Master will prepare us for the toil and hardships of the most strenuous campaign. We must, therefore, hold firmly and steadily to this primary principle, that of all things that need doing this need is supreme, to live in intimate fellowship with God. Let us steadily hold a reasonable sense of values, and assign each appointed duty to its legitimate place. And in any appointment of values this would surely be the initial judgment, that nothing can be well done if we drift away from God. Neglected spiritual fellowship means futility all along the road.

But the discipline of the soul must be

serious and studious. This high culture must
not be governed by haphazard or caprice.
There must be purpose and method and
regularity. And you may depend upon
it, that when you give yourselves to soul-
culture in this serious way, it is a travail
and not a pastime. If it were easy it might
scarcely be worth counselling: it is tre-
mendously difficult, but its rewards are
infinite. One of the most cultured spirits
in modern Methodism, a man whose style
is as strong as his thoughts are lofty, has
recently given this judgment as he looked
back upon the years of his ministry: " I
have not failed to study: I have not failed
to visit: I have not failed to write and
meditate: but I have failed to pray. . . .
Now why have I not prayed? Sometimes
because I did not like it: at other times
because I hardly dared: and yet at other
times because I had something else to do.
Let us be very frank. It is a grand thing to
get a praying minister. . . . I have heard
men talk about prayer who never prayed
in their lives. They thought they did:

but when you have heard them, they made their own confession in a ruthless way." These sentences lift the veil upon a naked experience, and they expose the solemn fact that prayer is very costly, even at the expense of blood, and that churches which have praying ministers may not realize the travail by which the power is gained. We are permitted to look upon our Master as He prays. "In the days of His flesh He offered up prayers and supplications with strong crying and tears." It was a holy and a costly business. "And being in an agony He prayed more earnestly, and His sweat was as it were great drops of blood falling down to the ground." There was something here which we can never share, and yet there is something which we must share if we are leagued with the Lord in the ministry of intercession, and enter into "the fellowship of His sufferings."

Perhaps I cannot better illustrate the costliness of this intensive soul-culture than by the example of Dr. Andrew Bonar.

Dr. Bonar laboured in Scotland a generation or two ago, and he adorned his ministry by a very saintly life and by very fruitful service. He kept a private diary or journal, contained in two small volumes, containing regular entries from 1828 to within a few weeks of his death in 1892. His daughter has permitted this most priceless record of a soul's pilgrimage to be given to the world, "in the belief that the voice now silent on earth will still be heard in these pages, calling on us as from the other world to be 'followers of them who, through faith and patience, are inheriting the promises.'"

Let me give you one or two extracts from this journal. "By the grace of God and the strength of His Holy Spirit I desire to lay down the rule not to speak to man until I have spoken to God: not to do anything with my hand until I have been upon my knees: not to read letters or papers until I have read something of the Holy Scriptures." . . . "In prayer in the wood for some time, having set apart three hours for devotion: felt drawn out much to pray for that peculiar fragrance which believers have about them, who are very much in fellowship with God." . . . "Yesterday got a day to myself for prayer. With me every time of prayer, or almost every time, begins with a conflict." . . . "It is my deepest regret that I pray so little. I should count the days, not by what I have of new instances of usefulness, but by the times I have been enabled to pray in faith, and to take hold upon God." . . . "I see that unless I keep up short prayer every day throughout the whole day, at intervals, I lose the spirit of prayer." . . . "Too much work without corresponding prayer. To-day setting myself to pray. The Lord forthwith seems to send a dew upon my soul." . . . "Was enabled to spend part of Thursday in the church, praying. Have had great help in study since then." . . . "Last night could do little else but converse with the Lord about the awakening of souls, and ask it earnestly." . . . "Passed six hours to-day in prayer and Scripture-reading, confessing sin, and seeking blessing for myself and the parish."

Words like these, written for no eye but God's to see, give deep significance to the sentence I quoted from our distinguished Methodist friend: " It is a grand thing to get a praying minister." And another thing becomes evident in the light of this journal: real prayer is the sharing of " the travail which makes God's Kingdom come." Andrew Bonar was a strong minister of " the grace of the Lord Jesus," and in the wrestling communion of prayer he became mighty with God and man. Men of his type, whose souls are elevated and refined by lofty fellowships, approach everything " from above," and not " from beneath." The trouble with many of us is just this,—we come to our work from low levels, from the common angle, with the ordinary points of view. In that way we come to our sermons, and to our pulpits, and to our pastoral work, and to the business affairs of the Church. We are " from beneath." We do not come upon our labours " from above," with the sense of the heavenly about us, with quiet feeling of elevation, and strong power of vision, and the perception of proportion and values. Men who are " from beneath" belittle and degrade the things they touch. Men who are " from above " elevate them, and give distinction and dignity to the meanest service. And if any minister is to live " in heavenly places in Christ Jesus," and to have this lofty bearing and this uplifting constraint in his common work, if he is to be pure and purifying, he must learn to " pray without ceasing."

And I would add one further word in reference to the discipline of character by the culture of the soul, and it is this: it is only by this primary culture that we gain those secondary virtues which play so vital a part in our moral defences, and in the effectiveness of our work. The fragrance of character usually rises from the apparently subordinate virtues, the very virtues which are commonly neglected or ignored. All the ten lepers had faith, only one had gratitude, and he is the one who remains beauteous and winsome in the regard of the Lord. And this very grace of gratitude fills a great part in a minister's life, and so do courtesy, and patience, and that wonderfully beautiful thing we call considerateness, and forbearance, and good-temper. I have called them secondary virtues, but I am afraid I have degraded their rank, so high and so princely a place do they fill in the shining equipment of the Christian ministry. And I name them here in order to reaffirm my conviction that such strong and attractive graces are not " works "; they are " fruits," the natural and spontaneous growth of much communion with the Lord. We may be fragrant in character, having " beauty " as well as " strength," if we abide in the King's gardens.

Gentlemen, I have mentioned our perils, and I have suggested our resources, and the one is more than sufficient for the other. A calling without difficulty would not be worth our choice. You will have traps and enemies, allurements and besetments, all along your way, but " grace abounds," and " the joy of the Lord is your strength."

THE PREACHER'S THEMES

"Feed my sheep"

LECTURE · THREE

THE PREACHER'S THEMES

"Feed my sheep"

I AM to speak to you to-day on the preacher's themes, and I have ventured to attach to the title the words of our Master, spoken to Simon Peter,—" Feed my sheep." I do not forget the particular conditions in which the counsel was born, but I believe that, without doing it any violence, it has immediate significance for our present meditation. The words are descriptive of a pastoral relationship, a shepherd caring for the needs of his flock. The shepherd is to lead his sheep from the barrenness of the wilderness, or from patches where the herbage is scanty and unsatisfying, to " green pastures " and " still waters." He is to watch against famine and drought. He is to " feed " his sheep, to " satisfy their mouth with good things."

And ours, too, is the pastoral relationship. A flock is committed to our care.

There are manifold duties connected with the office, but we are just now concerned with the primary responsibility of defending our sheep against the perils of hunger. To us is entrusted the solemn duty of finding food. The sheep are largely dependent upon their shepherds for the riches or poverty of their provisions. We are to provide against starvation, or against that semi-starvation which arises from innutritious herbage, and which results in weakness, anæmia, disease. We have the choice of the pastures. Where shall we choose?

To drop my metaphor, you and I are accounted responsible, by our very vocation, for the feeding of immortal souls. They will look to us for spiritual food. We are appointed to bring them satisfaction, to provide them with strong and wholesome nutriment by which they shall be competent to carry their daily burden, and to engage in life's battles without faintness or exhaustion. That is what you men are going out into the world to do. You are to be guardians of the church's health by pro-

viding against moral and spiritual famine.
You are to see to it that bread is at
hand by which the soul can be " restored."
When men and women come to your spiritual table, with aching cravings and desires,
they are to find such provision as shall
send them away with the words of the
Psalmist upon their lips: " He satisfieth
the longing soul, and filleth the hungry
soul with goodness "; " We shall be satisfied with the goodness of Thy house, even
of Thy holy temple! "

Now what shall we give them? What is
our conception of bread? To what aspects
of truth shall we lead the souls of men?
What shall be the marrow of our preaching? What shall be our themes? To what
clamant needs shall we address ourselves?
" Life," says a very wise observer, " grows
more and more severe. Pain becomes more
inward. Grief and strain advance along
with physical security and comfort. Civili-
zation only internalizes the trouble. We
have fewer wounds but more weariness.
We are better cared for but we have more

care. There is less agony, perhaps, but perhaps also, more misery." What " bread of life " shall we bring to lives so burdened and stricken? What shall we preach?

I suppose it will be the common judgment that in many quarters a great change has taken place in the character of pulpit themes, and in the treatment of them. Subjects are introduced to-day which would never have been considered even a generation ago. In many instances the subjects are not so much themes, in the sense of the presentation of great truths, but "topics," the consideration of some passing crisis, or of some local combinatior of circumstances, or of some incident which is exciting the attention of the daily press. Many reasons are given to account for this change.

In the first place it is said to be explained by a broader and healthier conception of the preacher's mission. We are told that it should be a preacher's ambition not only to have " a spirit of wisdom," but also " a spirit of understanding," not merely a knowledge of principles, but a skill in their practical application. He must be more than seer, he must be architect: he must be more than architect, he must be artisan. His preaching must do more than indicate ideal and goal, it must prepare the way by which the goal is reached. The preacher must be more than " a light to my path," he must be " a lamp unto my feet." All of which means that the preacher must be more than an idealist, more than a theologian, more than an evangelist: he must busy himself in the realms of political and social economics.

I have personally nothing to say in disparagement of these momentous ministries, and I deeply honour the men who are engaged in them. I very gratefully recognize the peculiarly special gifts and vision in which some men find their equipment and calling to this particular form of service. With equal readiness and gratitude I recognize the part which some men have played in the illumination of social ideals, in the disentanglement of social complexities, and in the inspiration of social service. But with all this you will permit me to express my own conviction as to the perils which beset a preacher in themes and ministries like these. I am in no doubt of my position as a citizen, and of my duties and privileges in the life of the nation. I must not be an alien to the commonwealth, living remote and aloof from its travails and throes. My strength must be enlisted in the vital, actual forces which, through tremendous obstacles, are seeking the enthronement of justice and truth. I can also conceive it probable that critical occasions may arise when it will be the duty of the pulpit to speak with clarion distinctness on the policy of the state or nation. But even with these admissions I can clearly see this danger, that the broadening conception of the preacher's mission may lead to the emphasis of the Old Testament message of reform rather than to the New Testament message of redemption. Men may become so absorbed in social wrongs as to miss the deeper malady of personal sin. They may lift the rod of oppression and leave the burden of guilt. They may seek to correct social dislocations and overlook the awful disorder of the soul. It seems to me that some preachers have made up their minds to live in the Old Testament rather than in the New, and to walk with the prophet rather than with the apostle and evangelist. Amazing differences are determined by a man's choice of central home; whether, say, he shall dwell in the gospel of John or in the Book of Amos, whether, say, in the wonderful realms of the epistle to the Ephesians, or in the smaller world of Isaiah or Jeremiah. It is all a matter of centre, of dwelling-place, of settled home. Where does a preacher live? From what place do his journeyings begin? To what bourn do his journeyings return? These are the central tests, and my observation leads me to think that the broader conception of the preacher's mission sometimes tends to lure him away to the circumference and suburbs of life, and to partially efface the vital,

tremendous verities of redeeming grace.
In the fascinating breadth we may lose
centrality: things that are secondary and
subordinate may take the throne.

Let me not be misunderstood. While I
write these words I carry in my mind the
memory of Dr. Dale, and the character of
his life and ministry. Now Dale was a
great politician, he was an intimate friend
and fellow-labourer of Gladstone and
Bright and Chamberlain. He burned with
the passion of righteousness. He entered
deeply into social, educational, and political questions, and he flung himself with
stern enthusiasm into every campaign for
the rectification of crooked conditions, for
the widening of the bounds of freedom, and
for the enrichment of the general life of
the nation. Yes, Dale was a great politician, but he was a greater preacher, and
the themes of his pulpit were vaster and
more fundamental than those he dealt with
on the platform. Was ever a pulpit de-
voted to mightier themes than when Dale
filled it! Turn to his book on " The

Atonement ": every chapter went through his pulpit! Take his incomparable work on Ephesians: it was all preached in his pulpit! Or look at his maturest work, the great book on " Christian Doctrine ": every word of it was given to his people through the pulpit! " I hear that you are preaching doctrinal sermons to the congregation at Carrs Lane," a fellow-minister said to him one day: " they will not stand it." Dale replied, " They will have to stand it," and throughout his long and noble ministry they not only stood it, but welcomed it, and rejoiced in it, and were nourished for the splendid service which that church has always rendered to the cause of civil and religious liberty. At the very time when he was foremost as a politician his pulpit was dealing with the awful yet glorious mysteries of redeeming grace. Dale's home was not among the prophets but among the apostles and evangelists. He visited Isaiah, but he lived with Paul. Nay, he dwelt " in heavenly places in Christ Jesus," and it was the glories of that lofty relationship, which he had obtained by grace, and at which he never ceased to wonder, that he sought to unveil Sunday by Sunday to his waiting people. His pulpit was reserved for vital and central themes: he never allowed the calls of wider citizenship to snare him from his throne.

There is another peril which I will name. The sense of scriptural truth is very delicate and it can be easily impaired. Every preacher knows how sensitive is the organ of spiritual perception, and how vigilantly it has to be guarded if he is to retain his vision and apprehension of "the deeper things" of God. You will find in your ministry that an evil temper can make you blind. You will find that jealousy can scale your eyes until the heavens give no light. You will find that paltry temper raises an earth-born cloud between you and the hills of God. You will find when you enter your study that your moral and spiritual condition demands your first attention. I have sat down to the preparation of my sermon and the heavens have

been as brass! I have turned to the gospel
of John and it has been as a wilderness,
without verdure or dew! Yes, you will
find that when your spirit is impaired, your
Bible, and your lexicons, and your com-
mentaries are only like so many spectacles
behind which there are no eyes: you have
no sight!

All this you will probably grant when
our attention is confined to the influence
of deliberate sin upon spiritual vision. But
I would ask you to consider whether the
spiritual organ of the preacher may not be
bruised if he is enticed to give the burden
of his attention to secondary discussion and
controversies, to matters which have certainly not first rank in the interests of the
soul. I believe it is possible for the soci-
ologist to impair the evangelist in the
preacher, and that a man can lose his power
to unveil and display " the unsearchable
riches of Christ." Gentlemen, this fear is
not the creation of the fancy. I have heard
men make the confession that they have
acquired a passion and aptitude for certain

[85]

types of preaching, and they have lost the power to expound those deepest matters which absorbingly engaged the heart and brain of the Apostle Paul. When the preacher becomes economist there are men outside who can surpass him in his office. His influence in these secondary realms is comparatively small. His legitimate and unshared throne is elsewhere and among other themes. It is for him to keep a clean, clear, true insight into the things that matter most, to explore the wonderful love of God, to delve and mine in the treasures of redemption, " to know nothing among men save Jesus Christ and Him crucified."

But a second reason is given why the themes of the pulpit should be more widely varied than those of a past generation. We are told that there is a tragic lapse of interest in the Church. The Church is now surrounded by a multiplicity of conflicting or competing interests. Modern life has put on brighter colours: it has become more garish, more arresting, more mesmeric. Society has become more enticing, and lures of pleasure abound on every side. And all this is making the Church seem very grey and sombre, and her slow, old-fashioned ways appear like a " one-horse shay " amid the bright, swift times of automobile and aeroplane! And therefore the Church must " hurry up " and make her services more pleasant and savoury. Her themes must be " up-to-date." They must be " live " subjects for " live " men! They must be even a little sensational if they are to catch the interest of men who live in the thick of sensations from day to day.

I can quite understand men who take this position, and I think they offer certain reasonable counsels which it will be our wisdom to heed. But on the other hand I think the road is beset with perils which we must heed with equal vigilance. The Apostle Paul recognized changing assortments of circumstances, and he resolved upon a certain elasticity, and he became " all things to all men " that he might " save some." But in all the elasticity of his relations he never changed his themes.

[87]

He moved amid the garishness of Ephesus, and Corinth, and Rome, but he never borrowed the artificial splendour of his surroundings and thereby eclipsed the Cross. No " way of the world " seduced him from his central themes. Wherever he went, whether to a little prayer-meeting by the river-side in Philippi, or amid the aggressive, sensational glare of Ephesus or Corinth, he " determined to know nothing among men save Jesus Christ and Him crucified." And I am persuaded that amid all the changed conditions of our day—the social upheavals, the race for wealth, the quest of pleasure, we shall gain nothing by hugging the subordinate, or by paying any homage to the flippancy and frivolity of the time. The Church is in perilous ways when she begins to borrow the sensational notes of the passing hour. One of the clearest and wisest counsellors of our time, a man who knew the secrets of men because he dwelt in " the secret place of the Most High," gave this straight counsel to the ministry a little while ago: " Against religious sensationalism, *outré* sayings, startling advertisements, profane words, irreverent prayers, the younger ministry must make an unflinching stand, for the sake of the Church and the world, for the sake of their profession and themselves." I do not think these words describe an imaginary peril. The peril is already at our gates; in some quarters it has been an actual menace to our worship, and here and there the menace has become a " destruction that wasteth at noonday." There is a certain reserved and reticent dignity which will always be an essential element in our power among men. We never reach the innermost room in any man's soul by the expediencies of the showman or the buffoon. The way of irreverence will never bring us to the holy place. Let us be as familiar as you please, but let it be the familiarity of simplicity, the simplicity which clothes itself in all things natural, chaste, and refined. And I think if we were to exercise ourselves upon things supremely beautiful we should find that we had hit upon the supremely sensational, and that the out-of-the-way themes, the glaring titles, the loud advertisements, are undesirable ministers in the quest and cure of souls.

What are the needs of the people who face us in the pews? In their innermost souls what do they crave? Are they hungering for the rediscussion of newspaper topics, with only the added flavour of the sanction of the sanctuary? Shall the preacher be just a visible editor, presenting his message amid the solemn inspirations of prayer and praise? What is the apostolic guidance in the matter? When I turn to apostolic witness and preaching I am growingly amazed at the fulness and glory of the message. There is a range about it, ana a vastness, and a radiance, and a colour which have been the growing astonishment of my latter years. When I turn to it I feel as though I am in Alpine country; majestic heights with tracts of virgin snow; suggestions of untraversed depths with most significant silence; mighty rivers full and brimming all the year round; fields of exquisite flowers nestling beneath the protecting care of precipitous grandeur; fruit-trees on the lower slopes, each bearing its fruit in its season; the song of birds; the moving air; the awful tempest. Turn to one of Paul's epistles, and you will experience this sense of air, and space, and height, and grandeur. Turn to Ephesians, or Colossians, or Romans, and you feel at once you are not in some little hill-country, and still less on some unimpressive and monotonous plain, you are in mountainous country, awful, arresting, and yet also fascinating, companionable, intimate. In Ephesians you lift your wondering eyes upon the ineffable Glory, but you also wander by rivers of grace, and you walk in paths of light, and you gather " the fruits of the Spirit " from the tree that grows by the way. I say it is this vastness, this manifold glory of apostolic preaching which more and more allures me, and more and more overwhelms me as the years of my ministry go by. There is something here to awaken the wonder of men, to lead them into holy awe, to brace their spirits, to expand their minds, and to immeasurably enlarge their thought and life.

And what is true of apostolic preaching has been true of all great preaching down to this very hour. Take Thomas Boston. We are told that his language was " tasked and strained to the utmost, to admeasure and to understand," when he spoke of " those redemptive blessings which meet all men's necessities . . . the full and irrevocable forgiveness of sins; reinstatement in the divine favour and friendship; the gift of the Holy Spirit in his enlightening, purifying, and peace-giving influences, turning men into living temples of the living God; victory in death and over death; the reception of the soul at death into the Father's house, and the beatific vision of God." These were the themes of transcendent interest which enriched and glorified the preaching of Thomas

[92]

Boston, and which made it so mighty a power for the highest good that there was scarcely a cottage home in all Ettrick in which some of his converts could not be found.

Or take Spurgeon. You may not like his theology. You may resent some of the phraseology in which his theology is enshrined. But I tell you that, with Spurgeon's preaching as your guide, your movements are not limited to some formal exercise on a barren asphalt area, or confined to the limits of some small backyard. Hear him on the love of God, on the grace of Christ Jesus, on the communion of the Holy Ghost. Hear him on such texts as "Accepted in the Beloved," "The Glory of His Grace," "The Forgiveness of Sins," "The Holy Spirit of Promise," "The Exceeding Greatness of His Power to Usward Who Believe"—hear him on themes like these, and you have a sense of vastness kindred to that which awes you when you listen to the Apostle Paul. Every apparently simple division in the sermon is like the turning of the telescope to some new galaxy of luminous wonders in the unfathomable sky.

Or take Newman. What was it that held the cultured crowds in St. Mary's enthralled in almost painful silence? I know there was the supreme genius of the preacher. There was also that mysterious fascination which always attaches to the mystic and the ascetic, to those who are most evidently detached from the jostling and heated interests of the world. But above and beyond these there was the vastness and the inwardness of the themes with which he dealt. His hearers were constrained from the study to the sanctuary, from the market-place to the holy place, even to " the heavenly places in Christ Jesus." The very titles of his sermons tell us where he dwelt: " Saving Knowledge," " The Quickening Spirit," " The Humiliation of the Eternal Son," " Holiness Necessary for Future Blessedness," " Christ Manifested in Remembrance," " The Glory of God." The very

[94]

recital of the themes enlarges the mind, and induces that sacred fear which is "the beginning of wisdom." The preacher was always moving in a vast world, the solemn greatness of life was continually upon him, and there was ever the call of the Infinite even in the practical counsel concerning the duty of the immediate day.

I say this has been the mood and the manner of all great and effective preaching. It was even so with the mighty preaching of Thomas Binney. "He seemed," says one who knew him well, " to look at the horizon rather than at an enclosed field, or a local landscape. He had a marvellous way of connecting every subject with eternity past and with eternity to come." Yes, and that was Pauline and apostolic. It was as though you were looking at a bit of carved wood in a Swiss village window, and you lifted your eyes and saw the forest where the wood was nourished, and, higher still, the everlasting snows! Yes, that was Binney's way, Dale's way, the way of

Bushnell, and Newman, and Spurgeon—
they were always willing to stop at the
village window, but they always linked
the streets with the heights, and sent your
souls a-roaming over the eternal hills of
God. And this it is which always impresses me, and impresses me more and
more—the solemn spaciousness of their
themes, the glory of their unveilings, their
wrestlings with language to make the
glory known, the voice of the Eternal in
their practical appeals; and this it is which
so profoundly moved their hearers to
" wonder, love, and praise."

Well now, is our preaching to-day char-
acterized by this apostolic vastness of
theme, this unfolding of arresting spiritual
wealth and glory? I ask these questions
not that we may register a hasty and careless verdict, but to suggest a serious and
personal inquiry. Dr. Gore, the Bishop
of Oxford, has been recently telling us
what he thinks is the perilous tendency of
the ministers and teachers of the Protes-
tant religion. He declares that we are

seeking refuge from the difficulties of thought in the opportunities of action. That is a very serious suggestion. It would mean that we are intensely busy in the little village shop, and have no vision of the pine forests, or of the august splendours of the everlasting hills. And it would mean something more than this. We are not going to enrich our action by the impoverishment of our thought. A skimmed theology will not produce a more intimate philanthropy. We are not going to become more ardent lovers of men by the cooling of our love for God. You cannot drop the big themes and create great saints.

But altogether apart from what Dr. Gore thinks of our preaching, what do we think of it ourselves? In the light of the example of the Apostle Paul, of his teaching and preaching, and by the example of the other great preachers I have named, how does it fare with our familiar themes? Are they always in the village shop, or is there always a suggestion of the mountains about them? Are they thin, and small, and of the dwarfed variety? Can our language very easily say all that we have got to say, or does it fail to carry the glory we would fain express? Is it not true that our language is often too big for our thought, and our thought is like a spoonful of sad wine rattling about in a very ornate and distinguished bottle? Men may admire the bottle, but they find no inspiration in the wine. Yes, men admire, but they do not revere; they appreciate, but they do not repent; they are interested, but they are not exalted. They say, " What a fine sermon!" not, "What a great God!" They say, "What a ready speaker!" and not, "Oh, the depth of the riches both of the wisdom and knowledge of God!"

It is this note of vastitude, this ever-present sense and suggestion of the Infinite, which I think we need to recover in our modern preaching. Even when we are dealing with what we sometimes unfortunately distinguish as "practical" duties we need to emphasize their rootage in the eternal. It is at the gravest peril that we dissociate theology and ethics, and separate the thought of duty to men from the thought of its relation to God. When the Apostle Paul, in the twelfth chapter of Romans, begins to be hortatory, preceptive, practical, it is because he has already prepared the rich bed in which these strong and winsome graces may be grown. Every precept in the twelfth chapter sends its roots right down through all the previous chapters, through the rich, fat soil of sanctification and justification, and the mysterious energies of redeeming grace. We employ a universe to rear a lily-of-the-valley. We need the power of the Holy Spirit to rear a fruit of the Spirit. We require evangelical grace if we would create evangelical patience. We require "the truth as it is in Jesus" if we would furnish even a truly courteous life. Ruskin says that if you were to cut a square inch out of any of Turner's skies you would find the infinite in it. And it ought to be that if men were to take only a square inch out of any of our preaching, they would find a suggestion which would lead them to " the throne of God and of the Lamb."

All this means that we must preach upon the great texts of the Scriptures, the fat texts, the tremendous passages whose vast-nesses almost terrify us as we approach them. We may feel that we are but pig-mies in the stupendous task, but in these matters it is often better to lose ourselves in the immeasurable than to always con-fine our little boat to the measurable creeks along the shore. Yes, we must grapple with the big things, the things about which our people will hear nowhere else; the deep, the abiding, the things that permanently matter. We are not ap-pointed merely to give good advice, but to proclaim good news. Therefore must the apostolic themes be our themes: The holi-ness of God; the love of God; the grace of the Lord Jesus; the solemn wonders of

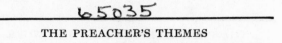

65035

the cross; the ministry of the Divine forgiveness; the fellowship of His sufferings;
the power of the Resurrection; the blessedness of divine communion; the heavenly
places in Christ Jesus; the mystical in-
dwelling of the Holy Ghost; the abolition
of the deadliness of death; the ageless life;
our Father's house; the liberty of the glory
of the children of God. Themes like
these are to be our power and distinction.
" O thou that tellest good tidings to Zion,
get thee up into the high mountain. O
thou that tellest good tidings to Jerusalem,
lift up thy voice with strength: lift it up:
be not afraid: say unto the cities of Judah,
Behold your God! "

If such is to be the weighty matter of
our preaching, we surely ought to be most
seriously careful how we proclaim it. The
matter may be bruised and spoiled by the
manner. The work of grace may be
marred by our own ungraciousness. We
may fail to grip and hold because of our
inconsiderate clumsiness. There are certain
things which it is necessary to avoid if we

would give even great themes directness
and wing. First of all, we must avoid a
cold officialism. There is nothing more
uncongenial to me, as I move about amid
the venerable stones and the subduing
presences of Westminster Abbey, than to
hear the cold, heartless, wonderless recitals
of the official guides. Yes, there is one
thing more uncongenial still, to hear the
great evangel of redeeming love recited
with the metallic apathy of a gramophone,
with the cold remoteness of an unapprecia-
tive machine. And that is our peril. The
world is tired of the mere official and is
hungry for the living man. It wants more
than a talker, it seeks the prophet. It
wants more than a sign-post, it seeks a
Greatheart who knows the ways of Zion,
who has found them in the travail of his
own soul, and who exults in their foun-
tains and flowers, and in all their exquisite
delights. The mere official spectralizes
the grandest themes, he offers men a
phantom deliverance and a phantom
feast.

"I've been to church," says Robert Louis Stevenson, in one of his letters, "I've been to church, and I am not depressed!" Walk down the suggestive lane of that phrase, and ponder its significance. "I once heard a preacher," says Emerson in a familiar passage, "who sorely tempted me to say I would go to church no more. A snowstorm was falling around us. The snowstorm was real; the preacher merely spectral, and the eye felt the sad contrast in looking at him, and then out of the window behind him, into the beautiful meteor of the snow. He had lived in vain. He had no one word intimating that he had laughed or wept, was married or in love, had been commended, or cheated, or chagrined. If he had ever lived and acted, we were none the wiser for it. The capital secret of his profession, namely, to convert life into truth, he had not learned." Yes, he was a mere official, wrenched from the innermost vitalities of his office. If he had ever had "the vision splendid," it had faded from his heaven, and no longer inspired his soul with light and flame. His words were only words, they were not spirit and life; he dwelt in the outermost courts of the temple, near to all the other traffickers in holy things—he was not a servant of the holy place, not a living priest of the living God. And his peril is our peril, subtle and insistent, the peril of remoteness from central issues, the peril of making substances appear shadows, and of making the holy splendours of grace seem like immaterial dreams. And, therefore, may we not fitly add to our private devotional liturgy an extra intercession, and may it not be this: " From all cold officialism of mind and heart; from the deadliness of custom and routine; from worldliness in which there is no spirit, and from ministry in which there is no life; from all formality, unreality, and pretence, good Lord, deliver us! " ?

And there is a second temptation which, if we yield to it, will impair the efficiency of even mighty themes, *the peril of dictatorialism.* I am not suggesting that we

are to affect a limp in our preaching, and
that we are to proclaim the word with
trembling hesitancy and indecision. But
there is a world of difference between the
authoritative and the dictatorial. In these
realms the authoritative messenger is
clothed with humility, the dictatorial messenger is clothed with subtle pride. One
walks on stilts, the other " walks in the
fear of the Lord." The dictatorial is self-
raised, the authoritative comes " from
above." And, therefore, the authoritative
carries an atmosphere as well as a message,
it has grace as well as truth. The dictatorial may have the form of truth, but
it does not carry the fragrance of the
King's garden; it lacks the grace of the
Lord Jesus. Now, I am perfectly sure
that here we find one reason why our
ministry is often so ineffective—we confuse
the dictatorial with the authoritative, plain-
ness with impressiveness, " straight speaking " with " speaking with tongues " as
the Spirit gives us utterance. We " call
a spade a spade," and think we have

spoken the truth. And so we dictate, but we don't persuade; we point the way, but few pilgrims take the road.

Look at the oppressive presence of sin. We may deal with it authoritatively or dictatorially. The weight of our speech may be derived from the tiny elevation of our office, or from the sublime heights of the " heavenly places in Christ Jesus." If we speak dictatorially we shall be only combatants: if we speak authoritatively we shall be saviours. If we are only dictatorial we shall speak with severity; if we are authoritative we shall speak with medicated severity, and men and women will begin to expose their poisoned wounds to our healing ministry. If we are only dictatorial our speech will have the aloofness of a prescription; if we are authoritative we shall have the immediacy of a surgeon engaged in the work of practical salvation.

Or take the dark and ubiquitous presence of sorrow. I have been greatly impressed in recent years by one refrain

which I have found running through many
biographies. Dr. Parker repeated again
and again, "Preach to broken hearts!"
And here is the testimony of Ian Maclaren:
"The chief end of preaching is comfort.
. . . Never can I forget what a distinguished scholar, who used to sit in my
church, once said to me: 'Your best work
in the pulpit has been to put heart into
men for the coming week!'" And may I
bring you an almost bleeding passage
from Dr. Dale: "People want to be comforted. . . . They need consolation—really
need it, and do not merely long for it. I
came to that conclusion some years ago,
but have never been able to amend my
ways as I wish. I try, and sometimes have
a partial success: but the success is only
partial. Four or five months ago I
preached a sermon on 'Rest in the Lord,'
and began to think I had found the
track: but if I did I lost it again. Last
Sunday week I preached on 'As far as
the east is from the west, so far hath He
removed our transgressions from us.'

That, I think, was still nearer to the right thing; but I cannot keep it up."

Brethren, if these men felt this need of the people, and also felt the difficulty of bringing their ministry to bear upon it, how is it with you and me? One thing is perfectly clear, the merely dictatorial will never heal the broken in heart, or bind up their bleeding wounds. Our power will not be found in our official rank, or in the respect paid to our vocation. Our power will be found in our authority, mysterious yet most real, an authority which is not the perquisite of human dignity or reward. We shall have to go to " the throne of God and of the Lamb," we shall have to tread the way which runs by the mystical river; we shall have to pluck the leaves of the tree which are for " the healing of the nations "; and with the exquisite tenderness of grace lay these leaves upon the wounds and the sorrows of our afflicted race.

And for all this tremendous but privileged task, which I have sought to out-

line in this lecture, the presentation of
great themes in a great way, ministering
to the sin, and sorrow, and weakness of
the world, we have the abundant resources
of a bountiful God. We have " the grace
of the Lord Jesus Christ, and the love of
God, and the communion of the Holy
Ghost "; and with these as our allies God's
statutes will become our songs.

THE PREACHER IN HIS STUDY
"A wise master-builder"

———

LECTURE · FOUR

THE PREACHER IN HIS STUDY

"A wise master-builder"

I AM to-day to ask your consideration to the subject of "The Preacher in His Study." What manner of man must the preacher be when he enters his workshop, and what kind of work shall he do? A little while ago I was reading the life of a very distinguished English judge, Lord Bowen, and in an illuminating statement of the powers and qualities required for success at the bar he used these words: "Cases are won in chambers." That is to say, so far as the barrister is concerned, his critical arena is not the public court but his own private room. He will not win triumph by extemporary wit, but by hard work. Cases are not won by jaunty "sorties" of flashing appeal, but by well-marshalled facts and disciplined arguments marching solidly together in invincible strength. "Cases are won in chambers."

And if a barrister is to practically conquer his jury before he meets them, by the victorious strength and sway of his preparations, shall it be otherwise with a preacher, before he seeks the verdict of his congregation? With us, too, "cases are won in chambers." Men are not deeply influenced by extemporized thought. They are not carried along by a current of fluency which is ignorant where it is going. Mere talkativeness will not put people into bonds. Happy-go-lucky sermons will lay no necessity upon the reason nor put any strong constraint upon the heart. Preaching that costs nothing accomplishes nothing. If the study is a lounge the pulpit will be an impertinence.

It is, therefore, imperative that the preacher go into his study to do hard work. We must make the business-man in our congregation feel that we are his peer in labour. There is no man so speedily discovered as an idle minister, and there is no man who is visited by swifter contempt. We may hide some things, but our idle-

ness is as obtrusive as though the name
of sluggard were branded on our fore-
heads. As indeed it is! And here we must
most vigilantly guard against self-deception. We may come to assume that we
are really working when we are only loaf-
ing through our days. The self-deception
may arise from many causes. I have
noticed that some people assume they are
very generous, but it is simply because they
have no system in their giving and no
record of their gifts. You will find, when
you get into your churches, that some people confuse the number of appeals they
have heard with the number of times they
have given; and the mere remembrance
of the appeals makes them sweat under the
burdened sense of their bounty. Their
self-deception is not intentional: it is only
consequential: they have very poor mem-
ories, and they use no system to aid them.
And so it is in respect to labour. If we
have no system we shall come to think we
were working when we were only thinking
about it, and that we were busy when we

were only engaged. And, therefore, with
all my heart I give this counsel,—be as
systematic as a business-man. Enter your
study at an appointed hour, and let that
hour be as early as the earliest of your
business-men goes to his warehouse or his
office. I remember in my earlier days how
I used to hear the factory operatives passing my house on the way to the mills,
where work began at six o'clock. I can
recall the sound of their iron-clogs ring-
ing through the street. The sound of the
clogs fetched me out of bed and took
me to my work. I no longer hear the
Yorkshire clogs, but I can see and hear
my business-men as they start off early to
earn their daily bread. And shall their
minister be behind them in his quest of the
Bread of Life? Shall he slouch and loiter
into the day, shamed by those he assumes
to lead, and shall his indolence be obtrusive
in the services of the sanctuary when " the
hungry sheep look up and are not fed "?
Let the minister, I say, be as business-like
as the business-man. Let him employ

system and method, and let him be as scrupulously punctual in his private habits in the service of his Lord, as he would have to be in a government-office in the service of his country. And to regularity let him add proportion. Let him estimate the comparative values of things. Let first things be put first, and let him give the freshness of his strength to matters of vital and primary concern. Gentlemen, all this will pay, and the payment will be made in sterling good. You will win the respect of your people, even of the most strenuous of them, and when they see that you " mean business " some of your obstacles will be already removed, and you will find an open way to the very citadels of their souls.

Now if this large, honest road is to be followed we shall go into our workshops for systematic study. We shall not be desultory or trifling. We shall not waste time in looking for work, but we shall begin to work at once. We shall not spend the early hours of the day in raking for texts, but in comprehensive visions of

truth. We must be explorers of a vast
continent of truth, and the individual texts
will find us out as we go along. Our very
insight into particular truths depends upon
our vision of broader truth. Our per-
ceptiveness is determined by our compre-
hensiveness. Men whose eyes range over
the vast prairies have intense discernment
of things that are near at hand. The
watchmaker, whose eyes are imprisoned to
the immediate, loses his strength of vision,
and soon requires artificial aid to see even
the immediate itself. The big outlook
makes you lynx-eyed: telescopic range gives
you also microscopic discernment. We
must study truth if we would understand
texts, as we should study literature to
understand the significance of individual
words.

How could you seize the significance of
such a phrase as " rejoicing in hope," or
" bless them which persecute you," found
in the twelfth chapter of Romans, unless
you see it drenched in the morning splendour of grace, and set in the radiant vistas

of the sanctified life? We cannot preserve the real life of these things if we cut them out, and detach them, and regard them as having no vital and infinite relations. The fact of the matter is, these practical counsels of the Apostle Paul are not added to his letters as though they were an unrelated appendix, casually bound up with matter with which they have no critical relation. Every counsel has blood-relationship to all that has preceded it. We require the entire letter for the understanding of only one of its parts. A duty in chapter twelve shines with a light reflected from chapter five, and it pulses with a motive and constraint which is born in chapter eight. The unveiled truth interprets and empowers the practical duty.

This is what I mean when I say that we are to be explorers of broad fields of revelation, and that we are to find our texts in these wide domains. I would, therefore, urge upon all young preachers, amid all their other reading, to be always engaged in the comprehensive study of some one book in the Bible. Let that book be studied with all the strenuous mental habits of a man's student days. Let him put into it the deliberate diligence, the painstaking care, the steady persistence with which he prepared for exacting examinations, and let him assign a part of every day to attaining perfect mastery over it. You will find this habit to be of immeasurable value in the enrichment of your ministry. In the first place, it will give you breadth of vision, and, therefore, it will give you perspective and proportion. You will see every text as coloured and determined by its context, and indeed as related to vast provinces of truth which might otherwise seem remote and irrelevant. And you will be continually fertilizing your minds by discoveries and surprises which will keep you from boredom, and which will keep you from that wearisome gin of commonplaces in whose accustomed grooves even the most stalwart grows faint. Wide journeyings and explorations of this kind will leave you no trouble about texts.

Texts will clamour for recognition, and your only trouble will be to find time to give them notice. The year will seem altogether too short to deal with the waiting procession and to exhibit their wealth. Yes, you will be embarrassed with your riches instead of with your poverty. I know one minister who, as he walked home from his church on Sunday nights, would almost invariably say to a deacon, who accompanied him, and say it with shaking head and melancholy tones, " Two more wanted! Two more! " He would send the eyes of his imagination roving over the thin little patch which he had gleaned so constantly, and he was filled with doleful wonder as to where he should gather a few more ears of corn for next week's bread! " Two more wanted! Two more! " He had no barns, or, if he had, they were empty! We must cultivate big farms, and we shall have well-stocked barns, and we shall not be moody gleaners searching for thin ears over a small and ill-cultivated field.

In your study you will, of course, take advantage of the best that scholarship can offer you in the interpretation of the Word. Before preaching upon any passage you will make the most patient inquisition, and under the guidance of acknowledged masters you will seek to realize the precise conditions in which the words were born. And here I want most strongly to urge you to cultivate the power of historical imagination: I mean the power to reconstitute the dead realms of the past and to repeople them with moving life. We shall never grip an old-world message until we can re-create the old-world life. Many of us have only a partial power, and it leaves us with maimed interpretations. To a certain extent we can refashion the past, but it is like Pompeii, it is dead. We get a setting, but not the life. Things are not in movement. We cannot transpose ourselves back with all our senses, and see things in all their play and interplay, and catch the sounds and secrets in the air, and touch the hurrying people in the streets, or nod to the shepherd on the hills. We may see the past as a photograph: we do not see it as a cinematograph. Things are not alive! And to see men alive is by no means an easy attainment. We cannot get it by reverie: it is the fruit of firm, steady, illumined imagination.

How are we to preach about Amos unless we can live with him on the hills of Tekoa, and see his environment as if it were part of our own surroundings, every sense active in its own reception: and unless we can go with him into Bethel, and note the very things that he sees along the road, and see the moving, tainted, insincere and rotten life which is congested in the town? How can we enter into the teaching of the Prophet Hosea unless by the power of a vividly exercised imagination we recover his surroundings? The Book of Hosea is filled with sights and sounds and scents. We must go back to his day and all our senses must be as open channels to the impressions that appealed to him. We must go with him along the streets, we must look into the houses and workshops. We must see the baker at his oven and kings and princes in their palace. We must walk with him through the lanes and among the fields at dawn of day when " the morn-ing cloud " is beginning to lift and the grass is drenched with " the early dew." We must see Hosea's homeland if we would intimately appreciate his speech. Or, again, how are we going to preach, say, about the Lord's tender ministries to the leper unless we can get into the leper's skin, and look out through his darkened windows, and shrink with his timidity, or come running with him along the highway, and in his very person kneel before the Lord? We must see that man, hear him, feel him: nay, we must *be* the man if we would know how to preach about the Mas-ter's words, " I will, be thou clean."

I am urging the cultivation of the his-torical imagination because I am persuaded that the want of it so often gives unreality to our preaching. If we do not realize the past we cannot get its vital message for the present. The past which is unfolded in the pages of Scripture is to many of us very wooden: and the men and the women are wooden: we do not feel their breathing: we do not hear them cry: we do not hear them laugh: we do not mix with their humanness and find that they are just like folk in the next street. And so the message is not alive. It does not pulse with actuality. It is too often a dead word belonging to a dead world, and it has no gripping relevancy to the throbbing lives of our own day. And so I urge you to cultivate the latent power of realization, the power to fill with breath the motionless forms of the past. If needful, before you preach upon an old-world message, spend a whole morning in hard endeavour to recall and vitalize the old world, until it becomes so vivid that you can scarcely tell whether you are a preacher in your study, or a citizen in some village, or city, or empire of the past.

Of course, you will consult other minds

upon your message, not that you may immediately accept their judgments, but that you may pass them through the mill of your own meditations. Indeed it is, perhaps, not so much their particular judgments that we need as their general points of view. One of the best things we can obtain from a man is not individualized counsels on particular problems, but the general standpoint from which he surveys the kingdom of truth. I know it is necessary to have much mental fellowship with a man before you gain this knowledge. It is easier to gather his opinions than to acquire his mental attitudes and inclinations. It is easier to pick up the verdicts of his mind than to become acquainted with its pose. But it can be done. We may come to know, with sufficient accuracy, how a man would approach a subject, how he would lay hold of it. Now I think it is an exceedingly enriching discipline to seek to look at our themes from other men's points of view. How would So-and-so look at this? By what road would he

approach it? One of our English maga-
zines has been lately propounding problems to its readers of this kind. One
week the readers were asked to identify
themselves with Dr. Johnson, with his
mind and heart and manner, and give his
probable opinions on Woman's Suffrage!
And I think some such similar discipline
must be employed in relation to our interpretation of the Word. If I may give
you my own experience, I have been in the
habit of following this practice for many
years. I ask,—how would Newman regard this subject? How would Spurgeon
approach it? How would Dale deal with
it? By what road would Bushnell come
up to it? Where would Maclaren take
his stand to look at it? Where would
Alexander Whyte lay hold of it? You
may think this a very presumptuous practice, and I have no doubt some of my conclusions would horrify the saintly men
whose heart-paths I have presumed to
trace. But here is the value of the practice,
it broadens and enriches my own concep-

tion of the theme, even though I may not have correctly interpreted the other men's points of view. I have looked at the theme through many windows, and some things appear which I should never have seen had I confined myself to the windows of my own mind and heart.

But while I am advising you to consult other minds I must further advise you not to be overwhelmed by them. Reverently respect your own individuality. I do not advise you to be aggressively singular, for then you may stand revealed as a crank, and your influence will be gone. But without being angular believe in your own angle, and work upon the assumption that it is through your own unrepeated personality that God purposes that your light should break upon the world. Reverently believe in your own uniqueness, and consecrate it in the power of the Holy Spirit. Be yourself, and slavishly imitate nobody. We do not want mimic greatness but great simplicity. When we begin to imitate we nearly always imitate the non-essentials, the tertiary things that scarcely count. In my own college there was a peril of our turning out a species of dwarfed or miniature Fairbairns. We could so easily acquire the trick of his style,—that sharp antithetical sentence, doubling back upon itself, and which we fashioned like standardized pieces of machinery cast in a foundry! I believe I became rather an expert in the process, and for some time I carried the Fairbairn moulds about with me, only unfortunately there was nothing in them! And so I counsel you not to borrow anybody's moulds of experience, and not to be intimidated by any other man's point of view. Consult him, be grateful for his judgments, but revere your own individuality, and respect the processes and findings of your own mind. You will find that the freshness of your own originality will give new flavour and zest to the feast which you set before your people.

When your subject is chosen, and you have had the guidance of all that sound scholarship can give you, and you have had

enriching communion with many minds, do
not feel obliged to preach upon the theme
on the following Sunday. It may be that
a word will lay hold of you so imperatively
as to make you feel that its proclamation
is urgent, and that its hour has come. But
I think it frequently happens that we go
into the pulpit with truth that is undi-
gested and with messages that are im-
mature. Our minds have not done their
work thoroughly, and when we present our
work to the public there is a good deal of
floating sediment in our thought, and a
consequent cloudiness about our words.
Now it is a good thing to put a subject
away to mature and clarify. When my
grandmother was making cider she used to
let it stand for long seasons in the sun-
light " to give it a soul!" And I think
that many of our sermons, when the preliminary work has been done, should be
laid aside for a while, before they are
offered to our congregations. There are
subconscious powers in the life that seem
to continue the ripening process when our

active judgments are engaged elsewhere. The subject " gets a soul," the sediment settles down, and in its lucidity it becomes like " the river of water of life, clear as crystal." Every preacher of experience will tell you that he has some sermons that have been " standing in the sun " for years, slowly maturing, and clarifying, but not yet ready to offer to the people. One of my congregation in Birmingham once asked Dr. Dale to preach upon a certain text in the epistle to the Romans, and he said he would seriously think about it. Long afterwards she reminded him of his promise, and she asked him when the sermon was coming. Dr. Dale answered her with great seriousness, " It is not ready yet! " At another time he was asked by another of his people to preach a course of sermons on some of the great evangelical chapters in the book of the prophecies of Isaiah. He made the same reply, " I am not ready yet." I came upon a similar instance in the life of Beecher. He was to preach at an ordination service

in New England. He said to Dr. Lyman
Abbott, " I think I shall preach a sermon
on pulpit dynamics; you had better look
out for it." " I did look for it," continued
Dr. Abbott, " and it was nothing but a
description of the incidental advantages of
the ministry as a profession. When I
next met Beecher I asked, ' Where is that
sermon on pulpit dynamics? ' ' It was not
ripe,' he replied."

The weakness of smaller preachers is
that their time is " always ready ": the
mighty preachers have long seasons when
they know their time " is not yet come."
They have the strength to go slowly and
even to " stand." They do not " rush into
print," or into speech, with " unpropor-
tioned thought." They can keep the
message back, sometimes for years, until
some day there is a soul in it, and a movement about it, which tells them " the hour
is come." Beware of the facility which,
if given a day's notice, is ready to preach
on anything! Let us cultivate the strength
of leisureliness, the long, strong processes

of meditation, the self-control that refuses
to be premature, the discipline that can
patiently await maturity. "Let patience
have her perfect work."

I have a conviction that no sermon is
ready for preaching, not ready for writing
out, until we can express its theme in a
short, pregnant sentence as clear as a
crystal. I find the getting of that sentence
is the hardest, the most exacting, and the
most fruitful labour in my study. To
compel oneself to fashion that sentence,
to dismiss every word that is vague,
ragged, ambiguous, to think oneself
through to a form of words which defines
the theme with scrupulous exactness,—this
is surely one of the most vital and essential
factors in the making of a sermon: and I
do not think any sermon ought to be
preached or even written, until that sentence has emerged, clear and lucid as a
cloudless moon. Do not confuse obscurity
with profundity, and do not imagine that
lucidity is necessarily shallow. Let the
preacher bind himself to the pursuit of

clear conceptions, and let him aid his pursuit by demanding that every sermon he
preaches shall express its theme and purpose in a sentence as lucid as his powers
can command. All this will mean that the
preparation of Sunday's sermons cannot
begin on Saturday morning and finish on
Saturday night. The preparation is a
long process: the best sermons are not
made, they grow: they have their analogies,
not in the manufactory, but in the garden
and the field.

I need not, perhaps, say that in all
the leisurely preparation of a sermon
we must keep in constant and immediate relation to life. The sermon is not
to be a disquisition on abstract truth, some
clever statement of unapplied philosophy,
some brilliant handling of remote meta-
physics. The sermon must be a proclamation of truth as vitally related to living
men and women. It must *touch* life where
the touch is significant, both in its crises
and its commonplaces. It must be truth
that travels closely with men, up hill, down

hill, or over the monotonous plain. And, therefore, the preacher's message must first of all " touch " the preacher himself. It must be truth that " finds " him in his daily life, truth that lies squarely upon his own circumstances, that fits his necessities, that fills the gaps of his needs as the inflowing tide fills the bays and coves along the shore. If the truth he preaches has no urgent relation to himself, if it does no business down his road, if it offers no close and serious fellowship in his journeyings, the sermon had best be laid aside. But the truth of a sermon must also make recognition of lives more varied than our own, and in the preparation of our sermons these must be kept in mind. I know that God " hath fashioned their hearts alike," and that the fundamental needs of men are everywhere the same: and yet there are great differences in temperament, and vast varieties of circumstances, of which we have to take account if our message is to find entry into new lives, and to have both attraction and authority. Perhaps

you will permit me to illustrate by men-
tioning my own plan. When I have got
my theme clearly defined, and I begin to
prepare its exposition, I keep in the circle
of my mind at least a dozen men and
women, very varied in their natural tem-
peraments, and very dissimilar in their
daily circumstances. These are not mere
abstractions. Neither are they dolls or
dummies. They are real men and women
whom I know: professional people, trading
people, learned and ignorant, rich and
poor. When I am preparing my work,
my mind is constantly glancing round
this invisible circle, and I consider how I
can so serve the bread of this particular
truth as to provide welcome nutriment for
all. What relation has this teaching to
that barrister? How can the truth be related to that doctor? What have I here
for that keenly nervous man with the
artistic temperament? And there is that
poor body upon whom the floods of sorrow
have been rolling their billows for many
years—what about her? And so on all

round the circle. You may not like my method: it probably would not suit you, and you may devise a better: but at any rate it does this for me,—in all my preparation it keeps me in actual touch with life, with real men and women, moving in the common streets, exposed to life's varying weathers, the "garish day," and the cold night, the gentle dew and the driving blast. It keeps me on the common earth: it saves me from losing myself in the clouds. Gentlemen, our messages must be related to life, to lives, and we must make everybody feel that our key fits the lock of his own private door.

With our purpose thus clearly defined, and keeping sight of actual men and women, we shall arrange our thought and message accordingly. There will be one straight road of exposition, making directly for the enlightenment of the mind, leading on to the capture of the judgment, on to the rousing of the conscience, on to the conquest of the will. This last sentence used figures of speech that are significant

of military tactics, and we do, indeed, require something of military strategy, in
its vigilance and ingenuity, in seeking to
win Mansoul for the Lord. How to so
expound and arrange the truth, along what
particular ways to direct it, so as to change
foes into allies and enlarge the bounds of
the Kingdom of Christ,—that is the problem that confronts the preacher every time
he prepares his sermon. And it may be,
it probably will be, that you will reject
outline after outline, outline after outline,
discarding them all as too indefinite and
uncertain, until one is planned which seems
to lead undeviatingly to the much-desired
end. First get your bare straight road,
with a clear issue: go no further until that
road is made: later on you may open
springs of refreshment, and you may
have even flowers and bird-song along
the way. But, first of all, I say, " Prepare ye the way of the people: cast up,
cast up the highway: gather out the
stones."

When all the preliminary labour is finished, and you begin to write your message, let me advise you not to be the bondslave to much-worn phraseology, and to forms of expression which have ceased to be significant. I do not counsel you to be unduly aggressive, and still less, irreverent, in your treatment of old terminology, but you will find amazing power in the newness of carefully chosen expressions, offered as new vehicles of old truth. A famous doctor told me that sickly people are often helped in their appetites by a frequent change of the ware on which their food is served. The new ware gives a certain freshness to the accustomed food. And so it is in the ministry of the word. A "new way of putting a thing" awakens zest and interest where the customary expression might leave the hearer listless and indifferent.

And in this matter of expression let me add one further word. Do not foolishly attach value to carelessness and disorder. Pay sacred heed to the ministry of style. When you have discovered a jewel give it the most appropriate setting. When you have discovered a truth give it the noblest expression you can find. A fine thought can bear, indeed it demands, a fine expression. A well-ordered, well-shaped sentence, carrying a body and weight of truth, will strangely influence even the uncultured hearer. We make a fatal mistake if we assume that uncultivated people love the uncouth. I have heard Henry Drummond address a meeting of "waifs and strays," a sombre little company of ragged, neglected, Edinburgh youngsters, and he spake to them with a simplicity and a finished refinement which added the spell of beauty to the vigour of the truth. There was no luxuriance, no flowery rhetoric: nothing of that sort: but the style was the servant of the truth, and, whether he was giving warning or encouragement, making them laugh or making them wonder, the sentences were "gentlemanly," a combination of beauty and strength.

And as for the illustrations we may

use in our exposition of a truth I have only one word to say. An illustration that requires explanation is worthless. A lamp should do its own work. I have seen illustrations that were like pretty drawing-room lamps, calling attention to themselves. A real preacher's illustrations are like street lamps, scarcely noticed, but throwing floods of light upon the road. Ornamental lamps will be of little or no use to you: honest street-lamps will serve your purpose at every turning.

Thus I conclude this consideration of " the preacher in his study." I need not remind you, after all I have said, that " a heavenly frame of mind is the best interpreter of Scripture." Unless our study is also our oratory we shall have no visions. We shall be " ever learning and never able to come to the knowledge of the truth." In these realms even hard work is fruitless unless we have " the fellowship of the Holy Spirit." But if our study be our sanctuary, " the secret place of the Most High," then the promise of ancient days shall be fulfilled in us, " the eyes of them that see shall not be dim, and the ears of them that hear shall hearken ": and the work of the Lord shall have free course and be glorified.

THE PREACHER IN HIS PULPIT

"The service of the sanctuary"

LECTURE · FIVE

THE PREACHER IN HIS PULPIT

" The service of the sanctuary "

I AM to speak to-day on the preacher's life and ministry in the pulpit. There is no sphere of labour more endowed with holy privilege and sacred promise, and there is no sphere where a man's impoverishment can be so painfully obtrusive. The pulpit may be the centre of overwhelming power, and it may be the scene of tragic disaster. What is the significance of our calling when we stand in the pulpit? It is our God-appointed office to lead men and women who are weary or wayward, exultant or depressed, eager or indifferent, into " the secret place of the Most High." We are to help the sinful to the fountain of cleansing, the bondslaves to the wonderful songs of deliverance. We are to help the halt and the lame to recover their lost nimbleness. We are to help the broken-winged into the healing light of

"the heavenly places in Christ Jesus."
We are to help the sad into the sunshine
of grace. We are to help the buoyant
to clothe themselves with "the garment
of praise." We are to help to redeem the
strong from the atheism of pride, and the
weak from the atheism of despair. We
are to help little children to see the glorious attractiveness of God, and we are to
help the aged to realize the encompassing
care of the Father and the assurance of
the eternal home. This is something of
what our calling means when we enter the
pulpit of the sanctuary. And our possible
glory is this, we may do it. And our
possible shame is this, we may hinder it.
When "the sick and the diseased" are
gathered together we may be ministers or
barriers to their healing. We may be
added encumbrances or spiritual helps.
We may be stumbling-blocks over which
our people have to climb in their desire to
commune with God.

Now we may not be able to command
intellectual power. Ours may not be the

gifts of exegetical insight, and luminous interpretation, and forceful and unique expression. We may never astound men by a display of cleverness, or by massive argumentative structures compel their admiration. But there is another and a better way at our command. With the powers and means that are ours we can build a plain, simple, honest altar, and we can invoke and secure the sacred fire. If we can never be " great " in the pulpit, when judged by worldly values, we can be prayerfully ambitious to be pure, and sincere, and void of offence. If the medium is not " big " we can make sure that it is clean, and that there is an open and uninterrupted channel for the waters of grace.

To this end I think it is needful, before we go into the pulpit, to define to ourselves, in simple, decisive terms, what we conceive to be the purpose of the service. Let us clearly formulate the end at which we aim. Let us put it into words. Don't let it hide in the cloudy realm of vague assumptions. Let us arrest ourselves in the very midst of our assumptions, and compel ourselves to name and register our ends. Let us take a pen in hand, and in order that we may still further banish the peril of vacuity let us commit to paper our purpose and ambition for the day. Let us give it the objectivity of a mariner's chart: let us survey our course, and steadily contemplate our haven. If, when we turn to the pulpit stair, some angel were to challenge us for the statement of our mission, we ought to be able to make immediate answer, without hesitancy or stammering, that this or that is the urgent errand on which we seek to serve our Lord to-day. But the weakness of the pulpit is too often this:—we are prone to drift through a service when we ought to steer. Too often " we are out on the ocean sailing," but we have no destination: we are " out for anywhere," and for nowhere in particular. The consequence is, the service has the fashion of a vagrancy when it ought to be possessed by the spirit of a crusade. On the other hand a lofty, single, imperial end knits together the detached elements in the service, it makes everything co-operative, and all are related and vitalized by the pervasive influence of the common purpose. "Who keeps one end in view makes all things serve." If the end we seek is "the glory of God" everything in the service will pay tribute to the quest.

Now let us see what this clearly formulated sense of sacred purpose will do for us. First of all, it will ensure the strong, gracious presences of reverence and order. Irreverence emerges when there is no sense of "the high calling." We "trample the courts of the Lord" when we lose our sight of the gleam. Unless we see "the Lord, high and lifted up," irreverent and disorderly things will appear in our conduct of the service. We cannot keep them out. We shall sprawl and lounge about the pulpit. We shall take little part in the worship we profess to lead. Our idle curiosity will be more

active than our spiritual obedience. We
shall be tempted to be flippant in tone,
to be careless in speech, and sometimes we
may be tripped into actual coarseness and
vulgarity. The first necessity to a refined
pulpit ministry is reverence, and if we are
to be reverent our eyes must be stayed
upon " The King in His beauty."

But let me mention a second security
which is attained when the service is domi-
nated by some great and exalted end. It
will defend the preacher from the peril of
ostentatious display. He will have power,
but it will not be an exhibition. He will
have light, but in the glory he himself
will be eclipsed. His ministry will be
transparent, not opaque. The vision of his
people will not be stayed on him, it will
gaze beyond him to the exalted Lord.
When I was in Northfield two years ago
I went out early one morning to conduct
a camp-meeting away in the woods. The
camp-dwellers were two or three hundred
men from the Water Street Mission in
New York. At the beginning of the serv-

ice prayer was offered for me, and the
prayer opened with this inspired supplica-
tion: "O Lord, we thank Thee for our
brother. Now blot him out!" And the
prayer continued: "Reveal Thy glory to
us in such blazing splendour that he shall
be forgotten." It was absolutely right and
I trust the prayer was answered. But,
gentlemen, if we ourselves are gazing upon
the glory of the Lord we shall be blotted
out in our own transparency. If we are
seeking the glory of the Lord there will
be about us a purity, and a simplicity,
and a singleness of devotion which will
minister to the unveiling of the King, and
men will "see no man, save Jesus only."
Everything in the service will be significant, but nothing will be obtrusive. Everything will meekly fall into place, and will
contribute to a reverent and sober setting in which our Lord will be revealed,
"full of grace and truth."

Now all this will mean a revolution in
the way in which some parts of the service are conducted. I would have you seri-

ously consider the pathetic, nay the tragic weakness of much of our devotional worship. We frequently fix our attention upon the sermon when we seek to account for the comparative impotency of a service, when perhaps the real cause of paralysis is to be found in our dead and deadening communion with God. There is nothing mightier than the utterance of spontaneous prayer when it is born in the depths of the soul. But there is nothing more dreadfully unimpressive than extemporary prayer which leaps about on the surfaces of things, a disorderly dance of empty words, going we know not whither,—a mob of words carrying no blood, bearing no secret of the soul, a whirl of insignificant expressions, behind which there is no vital pulse, no silent cry from lone and desolate depths.

It is not difficult to trace some of these weaknesses in pulpit prayer to their deeper cause. First of all, they are to be accounted for by our own shallow spiritual experience. We cannot be strong leaders of intercession unless we have a deep and growing acquaintance with the secret ways of the soul. We need to know its sicknesses,—its times of defilement, and fainting, and despair. We must know its cries and moans when it has been trapped by sin, or when it has been wearied with the license of unhallowed freedom. And we must know the soul in its healings, when life is in the ascendant, when spiritual death has lost its sting, and the spiritual grave its victory. And we must know the soul in its convalescence, when weakness is being conquered as well as disease, and life is recovering its lost powers of song. And we must know the soul in its health, when exuberance has returned, and in its joyful buoyancy it can " leap as an hart." How are we going to lead a congregation in prayer if these things are hidden from us as in unknown worlds? I confess I often shrink from the obligation, when I think of the richly-experienced souls whom I have to lead in prayer and praise. I think of the depths and the heights of their

[153]

knowledge of God. I think of their sense
of sin. I think of their rapture in the
blessedness of forgiveness. And I have to
be their medium in public worship for the
expression of their confessions, and their
aspirations, and their adoring praise! I
feel that I am like a shepherd's pipe when
they need an organ! They must often be
"straitened" in me in the exercises of
public communion. The preacher's shallow
experiences offer one explanation of the
poverty of his intercession.

But there is a second reason why our
public devotions are frequently so impoverished. It is to be found in our imperfect appreciation of the supreme and
vital importance of these parts of our services. They are sometimes described as
"the preliminaries," matters merely concerning the threshold, a sort of indifferent
passageway leading to a lighted room for
the main performance! I do not know
any word which is more significant of
mistaken emphasis and mistaken values,
and wherever it is truly descriptive

of our devotions the congregation, which looks to the pulpit for sacred guidance will find barrenness and night. It we think of prayer as one of " the preliminaries " we shall treat it accordingly. We shall stumble up to it. We shall stumble through it. We shall say " just what comes to us," for anything that " comes " will be as good as anything else! Anything will do for a " preliminary." We have prepared the words we are to speak to man, but any heedless speech will suffice for our communion with God! And so our prayerful people are chilled, and our prayerless people are hardened. We have offered unto the Lord God a " preliminary," and lo: " the heavens are as brass," and " the earth receives no rain."

And I would mention, as a third reason for the weakness and shallowness of public devotion, the preacher's lack of prayerfulness in private. If we are strangers to the way of communion in private we shall certainly miss it in public. The man who is much in "the way" instinctively finds the garden, and its fragrant spices, and its wonderfully bracing air, and he can lead others into it. But here, more than in anything else, our secret life will determine our public power. Men never learn to pray in public: they learn in private. We cannot put off our private habits and assume public ones with our pulpit robes. If prayer is an insignificant item in private it will be an almost irrelevant "preliminary" in public. If we are never in Gethsemane when alone we shall not find our way there with the crowd. If we never cry "out of the depths" when no one is near there will be no such cry when we are with the multitude. I repeat that our habits are fashioned in private, and a man cannot change his skin by merely putting on his gown.

I am fixing your thoughts upon this common weakness in pulpit devotions because I am persuaded it is here we touch the root of much of our pulpit incapacity. If men are unmoved by our prayers they are not likely to be profoundly stirred by our preaching. I cannot think that there will ever be more vital power in our sermons than in our intercessions. The power that upheaves the deepest life of the soul begins to move upon us while we commune with God. The climax may come in the sermon: the vital preparations are made in the devotions. I have heard pulpit intercessions so tremendous in their reach, so filled with God, so awe-inspiring, so subduing, so melting, that it was simply impossible they should be followed by an unimpressive sermon. The " way of the Lord " had been prepared. The soul was awake and on its knees, and the message came as the uplifting " power of God unto salvation." And on the other hand I have heard prayers so wooden, so leaden, so dead, or with only a show of life in loud tones and crude declamation, that it was simply impossible to have sermons full of the power of the Holy Ghost. I would therefore urge you, when you are in your pulpit, to regard the prayers as the essentials and not the "preliminaries" of the service, and to regard your sermon as a lamp whose arresting beams are to be fed by a holy oil which flows from the olive tree of sacred communion with God.

And there is a second "preliminary" in public worship which needs to be lifted into primary significance,—our reading of the word of God. Too frequently the Scripture-lesson is just something to be "got through." No careful and diligent work is given to its choice. No fine honour is assigned to it in the service. And the consequence is this, the "lesson" is one of the dead spots in the service, and its deadening influence chills the entire worship. The momentous message is given without momentousness, and it is devoid of even the ordinary impressiveness which belongs to common literature. How few of us remember services where the Scripture-lesson gripped the congregation and held it in awed and intelligent wonder! They tell us that Newman's reading of the Scriptures at Oxford was as great a season as his preaching. I know one man who always lights up the Burial Service by the wonderful way in which he reads the resurrection chapter in Paul's letter to the Corinthians. While he reads you can see and feel the morn dawning, even though you are in the home of the dead! You should have heard Spurgeon read the 103d Psalm! It is a mighty experience when a lesson is so read that it becomes the sermon, and the living word grips without an exposition. I said, " without an exposition." But there are expositions which are given in our manner, in our demeanour, in the very tones of our voice, in our entire bearing. I have been told that there was a fine and impressive homage in the way in which John Angel James used to open his pulpit Bible, and an equally subduing impressiveness in the way in which he closed it. These are not little tricks, taught by elocutionists: they are the fruits of character. If they are learned as little tricks they will only add to the artificiality of the service: if they are

" the fruits of the Spirit " they will tend to vitalize it.

If Scripture is to be impressively read it is of first importance that we understand it, that we have some idea of the general contour of the wonderful country, even though there are countless heights that we have never climbed, and countless depths that we have never fathomed. And if we are to have even this partial understanding of the lesson we must be prepared to give pains to it. I was deeply interested when I first went to Carrs Lane to examine Dr. Dale's copy of the Revised Version from which he read the lessons in his pulpit. It bore signs of the most diligent devotion. In difficult chapters the emphatic words were carefully marked, and parenthetical clauses and passages were clearly defined. Dr. Dale's making of an emphasis has sometimes been to me a revelation when I have read from his copy in the conduct of public worship. I mention this only to show what consecrated care one great expositor gave to the reading of the Scriptures. It is not elocution that we need, at least not the kind of elocution which in past years was given to theological students for the ministry. That was an imprisonment in artificial bonds which, for the sake of a galvanized life, destroyed all sense of weight and dignity. No, what we need, in the first place, is to exalt the ministry of the lesson in public worship, to set ourselves in reverent relationship to it, and then to give all needful diligence to understanding it and transferring our understanding to the people. Let us magnify the reading of the Word. Let us defend it with suitable conditions. Let us deliver it from all distractions. Let us keep the doors closed. Let no latecomers be loitering about the aisles while its message is being given. Let it be received in quietness, and it shall become manifest that God's word is still a lamp unto men's feet and a light unto their paths.

And now, in pursuit of the one exalted purpose of glorifying God in our pulpit

ministry, we shall give consecrated diligence to our common praise. Here again
we are touching something which may be
the abode of death or a fountain of resur-
rection-life. And here again we are turning to something to which many of us pay
but slight and indifferent regard. And
once again I am seeking to convey to you
the urgent conviction that every item in
the service carries its own effective significance, and that carelessness concerning any
part will inevitably lower the temperature
of the entire worship. I am perfectly sure
that it is with the hymns as it is with the
reading of the Scriptures; our heedlessness
is punished by antagonisms which make it
doubly difficult to reach our supreme end.
Many of the hymns we sing are artificial.
They are superficial and unreal. They
frequently express desires that no one
shares, and which no healthy, aspiring soul
should ever wish to share. Some of our
hymns are cloistral, even sepulchral, smell-
ing of death, and are far removed from the
actual ways of intercourse and the throb-

bing pulse of common need. The sentiment is often sickly and anæmic. It has
no strength of penitence or ambition. It
is languid, and weakly dreamy, more fitted
for an afternoon in Lotus-land than for
pilgrims who are battling their way to
God. And yet these hymns are indiffer-
ently chosen, and we use and sing them
with a detachment of spirit which makes
our worship a musical pretence. The thing
is hollow and devoid of meaning, and
through the emptiness of this "preliminary" we lead our people to the truth of
our message and hope that it will be received. It is a strangely unwise way, to
prepare for spiritual receptiveness by a
deadening formality which closes all the
pores of the soul. Every artificiality in
the service is an added barrier between the
soul and truth: every reality prepares the
soul for the reception of the Lord. The
hymn before the sermon has often aggra-
vated the preacher's task.

There is another matter which I should
like to mention in connection with our

hymns. Many of the hymns are char-
acterized by an extreme individualism
which may make them unsuitable for common use in public worship. I know how
singularly sweet and intimate may be the
communion of the soul with our Lord. I
know that no language can express the
delicacy of the ties between the Lamb and
His bride. And it is well that the soul,
laden with the glorious burden of redeeming grace, should be able to sing its
secret confidence and pour out the strains
of its personal troth to the Lord. " He
loved *me,* and gave Himself for *me!* "
But still I think that these hymns of intense individualism should be chosen with
prayerful and scrupulous care. Public
worship is not a means of grace wherein
each may assert his own individuality and
help himself from the common feast: it is
a communion where each may help his
brother to " the things which the Lord hath
prepared for them that love Him." A congregation is not supposed to be a crowd of
isolated units, each one intent upon a per-

sonal and private quest. The ideal is not
that each individual should hustle and bustle
for himself, stretching out his hand to touch
the hem of Christ's garment, but that each
should be tenderly solicitous of every other,
and particularly mindful of those with
" lame hands " who are timid and despond-
ent even in the very presence of the great
Physician. And so the ideal hymn in public worship is one in which we move together as a fellowship, bearing one another's
sins, sharing one another's conquests,
" weeping with them that weep, and rejoicing with them that rejoice."

In this wealth of widest sympathy we
must select our hymns. There must be a
hymn in which the sorrowful will lay his
burden, and the joyful will help him to lift
it. There must be a hymn for those who
are " valiant for the truth," and the timid
and the fearful may take courage while
they sing it. There must be a hymn in
which the newly-made bride shall see the
sacred light of her own new day, and the
newly-made widow will catch the beams of

the eternal morn. There must be hymns in which old people and little children can meet together and see the beauty of the leaf that never withers, and the glory of the abiding spring. All this means that our hymns cannot be chosen at the last moment if they are to be vital factors in a living service. They will have to be diligently considered, and their content carefully weighed, and we shall have to estimate their possible influence upon the entire worship. Do you not feel the reasonableness of this, and the importance of it, if every hymn is to be a positive ministry in constraining the congregation to intimate fellowship with God?

But even now I have not done with the musical portion of our worship. I want to urge you to cultivate friendship and most intimate communion with your organist. Enlist his spirit in your own exalted purpose. Make him realize, by the fellowship of your deepest desires, that he is a fellow-labourer in the salvation of men to the glory of God. Let the music be redeemed from being a human entertainment, and let it become a divine revelation. Let it never be an end in itself but a means of grace, something to be forgotten in the dawning of something grander. Let it never be regarded as an exhibition of human cleverness but rather as a transmitter of spiritual blessings: never a terminus, but always a thoroughfare. And therefore take counsel with your organist. Tell him what you want to do next Sunday. Do not be shy about leading the conversation into the deeper things. Do not keep him in the outer courts: take him into the secret place. Tell him your purpose in reference to each particular hymn, and what influence you hope it will have upon the people. Tell him what you are going to preach about, and lead him into the very central road of your own desires. Tell him you are going in quest of the prodigal, or to comfort the mourner, or to rouse the careless, or to encourage the faint. Tell him what part of the vast realm of "the unsearchable riches" you will seek to unveil to your people, and let his eyes be filled with the glory which is holding yours. Take counsel as to how he can co-operate with you, and let there be two men on the same great errand. Let him consider what kind of organ voluntaries will best minister to your common purpose and prepare the hearts of the people for the vision of God. Let a tune be chosen from the standpoint of what will best disclose the secret wealth of a hymn and open the soul to its reception. Never let the anthem be an "unchartered libertine," playing its own pranks irrespective of the rest of the service,—at the best an interlude, at the worst an intolerable interruption and antagonism—but let the anthem be leagued to the dominant purpose, urging the soul in the one direction, and preparing "the way of the Lord." In all these simple suggestions I am offering you counsel of incalculable worth. A preacher and his organist, profoundly one in the spirit of the Lord Jesus, have inconceivable strength in the ministry of redemption.

And indeed what I have said about the organist I would say concerning everybody who has any office in the service of the sanctuary. Let it be your ambition to make them co-operate in the purpose that possesses you. Your pulpit ministry is helped or hindered by everybody who has to deal with your congregation, even to the " doorkeeper in the house of the Lord." And, therefore, let your ushers know that they may be your fellow-labourers, not merely showing people to their seats, but by the spirit and manner of their service helping them near to God. Let every one of your helpers be on the inside of things, and in their very service worshipping God " in spirit and in truth."

Gentlemen, there is nothing petty or priggish in all this. A prig is a man who has never seen or has lost the august, and who is, therefore, swallowed up in his own conceit. I am seeking to depict a preacher who lives in the vision of the august, and who desires to lift into its splendour even the obscurest ministry of the sanctuary. There are portions of our services that are vagrant, unharnessed to the central purpose, and I want to recover their power to the direct mission of the salvation of men,—and it can only be done when the minister takes his fellow-workers into his counsels, and makes them at home in the secret desires of his own soul. We must cease to regard the sermon as the isolated sovereign of the service, and all other exercises as a retinue of subordinates. We must regard everything as of vital and sacred importance, and everything must enter the sanctuary clothed in strength and beauty.

And so with these mighty allies of prayer, and Scripture, and music, all pulsing with the power of the Holy Ghost, we shall give to a prepared people the message of the sermon. There are some questions about the sermon on which I am comparatively indifferent. Whether it shall be preached from a full manuscript or from notes, whether it shall be read, or delivered with greater detachment; these questions do not much concern me. Either method may be alive and effective if there be behind it a " live " man, real and glowing, fired with the passion of souls. Our people must realize that we are bent on serious business, that there is a deep, keen quest in our preaching, a sleepless and a deathless quest. They must feel in the sermon the presence of " the hound of heaven," tracking the soul in its most secret ways, following it in the ministry of salvation, to win it from death to life, from life to more abundant life, " from grace to grace," " from strength to strength," " from glory to glory."

And in all our preaching we must preach for verdicts. We must present our case, we must seek a verdict, and we must ask for immediate execution of the verdict. We are not in the pulpit to please the fancy. We are not there even to inform the mind, or to disturb the emotions, or to sway the judgment. These are only preparatives along the journey. Our ultimate object is to move the will, to set it in another course, to increase its pace, and to make it sing in "the ways of God's commandments." Yes, we are there to bring the wills of men into tune with the will of God, in order that God's statutes may become their songs. It is a blessed calling, frowning with difficulty, beset with disappointments, but its real rewards are "sweeter than honey and the honeycomb." There is no joy on earth comparable to his who has gone out with the great Shepherd, striding over the exposed mountain, and through deep valleys of dark shadow, seeking His sheep that was lost: no joy, I say, comparable to his when the sheep is found, and the Shepherd lays it on His shoulder rejoicing, and carries it home to the fold. "Rejoice with Me, for I have found My sheep which was lost!" And every one who has shared in the toil of the seeking shall also share in the joy of the finding—" Partaker of the sufferings " he shall also be " partaker of the glory." He shall assuredly " enter into the joy " of his Lord.

THE PREACHER IN THE HOME

"From house to house"

LECTURE · SIX

THE PREACHER IN THE HOME

"From house to house"

IN our previous lectures we have been considering the preacher's calling, the glory of his themes, the studious preparation of his message, and the presentation of the message in the sanctuary amid conditions which have been ordered and fashioned to be allies of the truth. And now we are to consider the preacher's calling when he leaves the public sanctuary and enters the private home. There is a change of sphere but no change of mission. The line of purpose continues unbroken. He is still a messenger, carrying good news; he is still an ambassador, bearing the decrees of the eternal God. His audience is smaller, his business is the same.

Now the difficulty of delivering a message is in inverse proportion to the size of the audience. The greater the audience the easier the task: with a diminished audience our difficulties are increased. I know that a crowd brings its perils, and they are very subtle, and we are not always doing our strongest work when we are least conscious of the dangers. Crowds may add to our comfort but they do not necessarily add to our spiritual triumphs. We may be least effective when we feel our work to be easiest, and we may be in the most deadly grips with things when we have difficulties and reluctances on every side. Now, I think that the common experience is this, that the difficulties of the messenger become multiplied as his hearers become few. It is a harder thing to speak about our Lord to a family than to a congregation, and it is harder still to single out one of the family and give the message to him. To face the individual soul with the word of God, to bring to him the mind of the Master, whether in counsel or encouragement, in reproof or comfort, is one of the heaviest commissions given to our charge. Where there are ten men who can face a crowd there is only one who can face the individual. What is the explanation of it?

Well, in the first place, the fear of a man is a much more subtle thing than the fear of men. The fear of a man bringeth a most insidious snare, and too often the fear is created by the mere accidents of circumstance and not by any essential gifts of character. We are intimidated by the office rather than by the officer: by a man's talents rather than by his disposition: by his wealth rather than by his personality. Nay, our timidity sometimes arises from the splendour of a man's house rather than from any splendour in the tenant. And from all this kind of fear the preacher is not exempt. The snare is ever about him, and he may measure his growth in grace by the strength with which he meets the snare and overcomes it. It was a noble type of courage which inspired Paul to "fight with beasts at Ephesus": it was a nobler courage with which he confronted the Apostle Peter, reputed to be "a pillar

of the Church," and " withstood him to the
face because he stood condemned."

I confess that this part of our commission, the carrying of the message to the
individual, was the greatest burden of my
early ministry. Of course it is perfectly
natural that in our earliest ministry this
burden should be the heaviest. There is
our lack of experience, there is the timidity
of untried powers, there is the deference
we pay to years,—all these tend to make
us fearful and reserved, and disinclined to
speak to individuals of their personal relationship to the Lord. A sermon is easier
than a conversation. And yet from the
very beginning of our ministry this obligation is laid upon us, and we cannot neglect
it without imperilling the health and wel-
fare of immortal souls. And how we
shrink from it! I vividly remember the
first battle-royal I had with the temptation
soon after my ministry began. I heard on
excellent authority that one of my people
was " giving way to drink." He was a
man of some standing in the church, and

he was possessed of considerable wealth. I
had already preached more than one tem-
perance sermon, but these had been general messages addressed to a congregation. I was now ordered by the Master to
carry the message to an individual, and to
tactfully withstand him to his face, because he stood condemned! How I wrig-
gled under the commission! How I shrank
from it! How I dallied with it! And
even when I had fought my way almost
to his door, I lingered in the street in
further faithless loitering. But at length
courage conquered fear, I faced my man,
tremblingly gave him my message, and by
the grace of God he heard the voice of
God and was saved from a horrible pit
and the miry clay. Gentlemen, it seemed
as though I could preach a sermon and
never meet a devil: but as soon as I began
to take my sermon to the individual the
streets were thick with devils, and I had
to be like the armed man in " The Pil-
grim's Progress " who, " after he had received and given many wounds to those

that attempted to keep him out, cut his way through them all, and pressed forward into the palace." But I will say again, " the fear of man bringeth a snare."

But there is perhaps a second reason why we shrink from these individual commissions. There is a certain secularity which is often embedded in our characters and which makes us half-ashamed to " talk religion " in private. The " wares " seem out of place. We can " talk " politics, or business, or sport, but religion seems an intrusion which will certainly be resented. Men can scent " the garments of myrrh " afar off, and turn away as they approach. And the secularity in our souls takes sides with this aversion, and we are snared into sinful silence, and our solemn charge is unfulfilled. And thus the spirit of the world makes its home in our souls and defines the limits of our commission. The Lord issues the decree, but worldliness is permitted to appoint its bounds.

And I will mention a third reason why the individual ministry is beset by so much reluctance and timidity. There is a certain shyness which makes us shrink from any assumption of moral and spiritual superiority. When we minister in the pulpit, and proclaim the exacting commandments of the Lord, we may regard the proclamation as the utterance of a voice not our own, and we may place ourselves among the struggling, stumbling congregation, which is listening to decrees from the great white throne. We can preach to a crowd and yet number ourselves in its faltering ranks. But when we go to the individual, to minister in the things of the higher life, we go not merely as a voice but as an incarnation. We cannot hide from ourselves that we go not only with the strength of a message but in the assumption of an attainment. And sometimes we shrink from it, lest the assumption should appear presumption, and lest we should seem tainted with Pharisaic pride and profession. That is an exceedingly subtle temptation. It is born amid the delicate reserves and reticences of true humility, but it may be perverted into the faithlessness of unlawful shame. It is one thing to be humble about our spiritual attainments, it is quite another thing to be betrayed into acting as though we had no tokens of heavenly favour, and no riches from the treasury of grace. There is a false modesty which makes us disloyal: there is a true humility which constrains us to make our boast in the Lord. The one may make us silent about ourselves, the other will make us silent about the Lord.

There may be other explanations, besides those which I have named, why many of us are so indisposed to religious dealings with the individual man. But whatever the radical explanation may be, there is the fact: we fear the individual more than we fear the crowd. Multitudes of ministers can fish with a net who are very reluctant to fish with a line. But it is as clearly a part of our commission to go out after " the one " as to minister to " the ninety-and-nine ": and therefore we are called upon to master our reluctance and our timidities, and with steady loyalty to carry our ministry from the pulpit into the home, and from the great assembly to the individual soul.

Now I want to frankly confess my own conviction that in this attempted ministry to the home there is a pathetic waste of precious time. I have no confidence whatever in the ministry which calculates its afternoon's work by the number of doorbells it has rung, and the number of streets it has covered, and the number of supposed " calls " that can be registered in the pastoral books. I attach little value to the breathless knocking at a door, the restless, " How do you do? " and the perspiring departure to another door where a similar hasty errand is effected. I attach even less value to a sharp, short series of afternoon gossipings which only skim the surfaces of things, and which never come within sight of those stupendous heights and depths that matter everything to immortal souls. " Wandering about from house to house . . . tattlers also and busybodies, speaking things which they ought

[185]

not." I say that this kind of ministry, burdensome and tiring as it certainly is, is effeminate work, and it is a tragic waste of a strong man's time. But here again, a clear and well-defined purpose, large, luminous, sacred, and sanctifying, will be our sure defence against puerilities and against all sinful trifling with time and strength. Ever and everywhere, in the pulpit and out of it, amid a crowd, with a few, or holding fellowship with the individual, the true minister will guide himself with the self-arresting challenge:— " What am I after? " and he will continually refresh his vision and ambition by the contemplation of the apostolic aim:— " To present every man perfect in Christ Jesus."

There is no need that a minister be pietistic just because he unceasingly cherishes a glorious end. Nay, the pious prig will be absolutely impossible where a man seeks to live in the glory of his " high calling in Christ Jesus." A lofty purpose can minister through lighter moods. It can consecrate church-bells and ring out a merry peal, as well as fire-bells and ring out its loud alarm. It can seek its serious ends through laughter as well as through tears. Its quest of the Holy Grail runs through many a bright and jocund day. It can use the ministries of wit and humour and yet never lose sight of its end. How true all this was of Spurgeon! He could fish in the sunniest seas! His geniality was ever the companion of his piety, and his smile was never far away from his tears. He followed a great purpose, and a big retinue of powers moved in his train. They moved with him in private as well as in public, when he communed with the individual and when he ministered to the crowd. And equally true was all this of Moody. He was a child of light, luminously human in the service of the divine, all the more human because he increasingly sought the glory of God. He moved and won men by his naturalness. He could throw his line through wit and humour, but in the central heart of all his merri-

ment there was a holy place where nothing
dwelt that was common or unclean. And
so, I say, a minister need not be a Stiggins
—a melancholy Stiggins because his life
is possessed of a lofty and serious end.
On the other hand, let his life lose its
holy and well-defined purpose, and there
is no man who will so surely drivel into
effeminacies, into idle puerilities, into
empty gossipings, into petty conventions
devoid of spiritual significance,—with the
added tragedy that he may come to be
satisfied with his barren lot.

When, then, we leave our pulpit, and on
the one sacred quest seek communion with
the individual, what can we do for him?
First of all, we can bring to a man *the
ministry of sympathetic listening.* You
will find that sometimes this is all that a
man requires, a sympathetic audience. It
is not that he needs your speech: he needs
your ears. " When I kept silence my
bones waxed old." Unshared troubles
bring on premature age. The trouble we
can talk about loses some of its weight.

An audience brings to many people a simplification of their grief. A strange light often breaks upon us when we are unfolding our troubles to another. When we begin to explain our difficulties we often explain them away. The problem is unravelled even while it is being described. You will find that this principle operates in the pulpit. While you are attempting to expound the truth to others you will see it yourself in clearer light. Things become luminous while they are being shared. They become transparent in fellowship. Our audience enriches our possessions. Now many people lack the audience and therefore they never come to their own. And we provide them with an audience, and our ministry to the individual is frequently just this provision of fellowship, the offer of an opportunity through which a soul can " speak " its way into light and liberty.

Think how many haunting fears vanish away when we try to put them into words.' Their strength is in their vagueness.

They are terrible because they are ill-defined. They are often banished by expression. We seek to put them into expression and they are gone! A fear thus shared is very frequently a fear destroyed. How often I have had that experience in my ministry! I have sat and listened to men and women as they have poured out the story of their griefs and fears. Scarcely a word has passed my lips. I seemed to be doing nothing, but it may be that in such ministries more sacred energies are at work than we have conceived. Who knows what mystic powers are operative when two souls are in sympathetic relation, and one is apparently passively listening to the tale of the other's woes? At any rate I have often been the silent partner in such fellowship, and often when I have come away the afflicted soul has said to me, " I cannot tell you how much you have helped me ": and I could see that by the mysterious workings of God's grace the yoke had been made easy and the burden light.

And so the minister provides the individual with an audience, but not only for the expression of trouble, and difficulty, and fear, but also for the transfiguration and enrichment of his joy. For joy that is never shared is never fully matured. A joy that tells its story is like some imprisoned bird that has found the sunny air of larger spaces. It is strengthened and vitalized, and it discovers new powers of rapture and song. Here again the audience enriches the songster by giving him occasion to sing. There are people who are laden with providential experiences, and they would become all the wealthier if they told their own simple story of grace. "This poor man cried, and the Lord heard him, and saved him out of all his troubles," but he would be all the richer just to tell his minister this chapter in the Lord's dealings with his soul. We strengthen a man's faith when we give him opportunity of confession: we enrich his joy when we listen to his song in the Lord.

But there is another side to this individual ministry. We are called upon by our God to bring to men not merely the strengthening grace of sympathetic listening, but also *the strengthening grace of sympathetic speech.* What can we say to a man when we meet him face to face? Our God will inspire the counsel if we will cherish and seek His glory. He will appoint the means if we will revere His ends. If I will follow " the light " upon my path He will "keep my feet." It is in ministries to the individual soul that the promise of our Lord has rich and immediate fulfilment:—" It shall be given you in that same hour what ye shall speak." Our discernments shall be made sensitive, our affections shall be kept sympathetic, our judgments shall be enlightened, and our words shall be as keys that fit the locks, and the " iron gate " in men's souls shall be opened. We need not trouble about the details of our approach to the individual if only our controlling purpose is clean and lofty.

What, then, shall be our sovereign purpose in moving among men in common affairs? It will surely be to relate the common to the divine, and to bring the vision of the sanctuary into the street and the market and the home. We are to go among men helping them to see the halo on the commonplace, to discern the sacred fire in the familiar bush. In the sanctuary men are frequently conscious of the stirrings of a heavenly air, but they lose its inspirations in the streets. In the sanctuary they often catch the gleam of the ideal, and they often feel the Sacred Presence of the Lord in the ways of public prayer and praise, but the gleam fades away when they touch their daily work, and the Sacred Presence is lost in the crowded roads of business. It must be our ministry to help them to recover their lost inheritance, and to retain the sense of heavenly fellowship while they earn their daily bread. We do a mighty work when we keep a man's sense of God alive amid all the hardening benumbments of the world. Sometimes a word will do it: sometimes even the word is not required. Ian Maclaren said that when Henry Drummond entered a room it seemed as though the temperature was changed. Everything looked and felt different, the medium of intercourse was brightened and clarified. Men's spiritual senses get jaded, they lose their fine perceptions, the setting of life becomes common and profane, and it may be our gracious ministry, by the vigour of our fellowship, altogether apart from actual speech, to " refresh " them, and to restore to them the lost sanctities. It may be we shall find some business-man living as though life were only a dreary and monotonous plain, and we may leave him " refreshed," having recovered the vision of " the hills of God." But it will also be our mission to recover the divine light, not only as it rests upon common labour, but as it rests upon the ordinary sorrows which so often appear sombre and hostile. That is a very beautiful ministry, one of the most gracious privileges committed to our hands. We are to go where the cloud is low, and black, and frowning, and we are to reveal its silver lining. We are to find " springs in the desert." We are to find flowers of divine mercy, forget-me-nots of heavenly grace, growing in the heaviest and ruttiest roads. We are to go into homes where sorrow reigns, and it is to be our tender ministry to show that Jesus reigns. We are to find " the Church in the wilderness." You will esteem this a very precious privilege, and you will esteem it more and more as the years pass by. You will lie down to sweet sleep on the days when you have lightened the path of the sorrowful, when you have shown the divine gleam resting upon the clod, and when the timid, riven heart has been quieted in the assurance that God is near.

I once called upon a cobbler whose home was in a little seaside town in the North of England. He worked alone in an exceedingly tiny room. I asked him if he did not sometimes feel oppressed by

the imprisonment of his little chamber.
" Oh, no," he replied, " if any feelings of
that sort begin I just open this door!"
And he opened a door leading into another
room, and it gave him a glorious view of
the sea! The little room was glorified in
its vast relations. To the cobbler's bench
there came the suggestion of the infinite.
And really, gentlemen, I think this expresses my conception of our ministry as
we encounter men and women in their
daily lot. We are to open that door and
let in the inspiration of the Infinite! We
are to go about skilfully relating everything to God:—the lowliest toil, the most
unwelcome duty, the task that bristles with
difficulty, the grey disappointment, the
black sorrow,—we are to open the door,
and let in upon them the light of the infinite purpose and the warm inspirations
of eternal love. It may be that sometimes the opening of that door may startle
and frighten a man rather than soothe
and comfort him. It may be that he is
deliberately keeping it closed, and in sinful

comfort he is living unmindful of God. Well, then, we must not shirk our duty. We must gently but firmly open the door even though the light should strike like lightning, and the man is filled with present resentment. The resentment will pass, it will most probably change into gratitude, and in the recovered vision of God the man will recover himself and all the riches and powers of his lost estate. For thus saith the Lord, " Son of Man, I have made thee a watchman unto the house of Israel: therefore hear the word at my mouth, and give them warning from me. When I say unto the wicked, Thou shalt surely die: and thou givest him not warning, nor speakest to warn the wicked from his wicked way, to save his life: the same wicked man shall die in his iniquity: but his blood will I require at thine hand. Yet if thou warn the wicked, and he turn not from his wickedness, nor from his wicked way, he shall die in his iniquity: but thou hast delivered thy soul."

Now let no one think that this ministry

to the individual is on our part an unmixed
expenditure, attended by no corresponding
returns. The personal recompense in
such labour is abundant. In the first
place we discover how strangely many are
the varieties of human experience. The
kaleidoscope of circumstances takes shapes
and fashions of which we ourselves have
never dreamed. And we shall find that
the changed assortment of circumstances
varies the conditions of warfare, and that,
while the general campaign of life for all
of us may be one and the same, the individual battles are never alike. Every
life has its own peculiar field, and we shall
discover conditions of warfare which we
have never shared. And then, in the
second place, through this variety and
multiplicity of human needs we shall more
gloriously apprehend the fulness and
glory of our resources in grace. We are
very tempted to interpret our own individuality as the common type, and to
express our message through the medium
of our own peculiar circumstances. It is

a minister's life that we see, and a minister's perils, and a minister's conflicts, and these are too often the settings of our sermons, and other men feel that they are living in another and alien world, and our counsels and warnings seem irrelevant. The ministry to the individual discovers the individuality of others, life breaks up into lives, each of its own fashion, and as we bring the common grace to the manifold needs our conception of grace is immeasurably glorified, " the same Lord over all being rich unto all that call upon Him."

Now, for this ministry to the individual mere book knowledge is of little or no service. Our knowledge must be personal, experimental, practical, and immediate. We need an experimental knowledge of God. There must be something solid and satisfying. *We must know something,* something about which we can be dogmatic, and about which we can speak in words and tones of assurance. " I know ": " I have felt ": " I have seen ": " I know

whom I have believed and am persuaded ":
—This must be the firm and confirming
assurance which fills our confession of the
grace and love of God. And to an experimental knowledge of God must be added
an experimental knowledge of the King's
highway. If Greatheart is to guide the
pilgrims from the City of Destruction to
the Celestial City he must know the road,
and he must be keen to recognize the
inviting and perilous by-paths which are
only flower-decked ways to destruction.
And for all this we need an intelligent and
experimental knowledge of the mysterious
workings of our own heart, of our own
inclinations and repulsions, and how in
our own souls the enemy has conquered or
been overthrown. And yet, with all this
we shall meet with problems in our individual ministry for which we have no
solution. We shall be asked questions to
which we have no personal reply. There
will be locks for which we have no keys.
How then? There is nothing more per-
nicious for a minister and for his people

than for him to assume knowledge and certainties which he does not possess. We discourage our people when we speak lightly and airily about heights that we have never climbed, and when we move with an air of familiarity in regions where we have no light. The best help you can offer some men is to tell them that you share their doubt and fear, and that the door at which they are knocking has never been opened to you. Let them feel your kinship in uncertainty where uncertainty reigns, and make no pretence of cloudless noon where there are only the doubtful rays of uncertain dawn. We are harmful in our ministry when we profess experiences which to ourselves and to others are only in the region of alluring dreams. When you are certain speak in faith, " nothing wavering ": when you are uncertain, when the light is still dubious, speak like a man who is watching for the morning: " For we know in part, and we prophesy in part ": and concerning the things we know not it is a minister's wisdom and piety to confess his ignorance, and to calmly and hopefully await the further unveiling.

In all that I have said to you in this lecture I have assumed that in your intercourse with men you will act as " the friend of the Bridegroom." You are about His most sacred business, seeking to win the soul to the Lord, and to minister to the holy relationships of Bridegroom and bride. That is our business, and we must, therefore, be regularly watchful lest any mood or disposition of ours should give a false impression of the Bridegroom and scare away the prospective bride. It is needful that we be jealously careful lest the impression we give in the pulpit should be effaced when we get into the home. " Jesting, which is not convenient," is never friendly to the Bridegroom. Spiritual moods are very sensitive, as sensitive and delicate as the awakenings of early love. Can you think of anything more exquisite than the love of a young girl, a love newly born in her soul, which she hides almost from herself, and in the most intense shyness shrinks from giving it expression? I know of only one thing more exquisite still,—the earliest mood of the soul when it is first "falling in Love" with the Lord. Yes, "the soul's awakening" is more exquisite still. And this love for the Bridegroom can be checked and bruised by the Bridegroom's friend; he can change its vision into fancies, and he can pervert its dawning passion into a transient dream. But, on the other hand, he may, by Christian grace and courtesy, and by "the strength which God supplies," confirm the "heart's desire" of a would-be-lover until the soul, wooed by his message, and encouraged by his life, has become the consort of Him who is "the chief among ten thousand and the altogether lovely."

I close this lecture with personal witness as to the spiritual good which has come my way through ministering to sick and troubled people, and to those who were beaten and crippled by the way. All the

way along it has quickened and deepened
my communion with God. Soon after I
entered the ministry I was called upon to
visit the senior elder of my church, who
had been taken sick unto death. He had
been a noble and stately figure among us,
a certain old-world grace and courtesy re-
flecting the strength and dignity of his
soul. He had been a great friend of the
Master, and he had done his Master's work
in a great way. I saw him two or three
days before he died, when it was known
that the end might come at any time, and
I found he was enjoying Dickens' "Pick-
wick Papers"! I must have made some
remark about it, and he replied very simply that he had always been fond of Pick-
wick, and that he would not be ashamed,
when the Master came, to be found deep
in the enjoyment of such innocent humour.
I do not know what helpful ministry I
brought to him, but I know that he gave
to me a broadly human conception of
matured piety, which all along the way
has enriched my conception of the fruits

of the Holy Spirit. In a very recent day of my ministry I went to see a man who had cancer in the throat. Time after time I had communion with him and never did a word of complaint escape his lips. The disease got fiercer hold upon him, his voice sank to a whisper, and at last all power of speech ceased. The first time I saw him after he had become dumb, he took a slip of paper and wrote these words upon it, " Bless the Lord, O my soul, and forget not all His benefits! " Again I say I know not what help I brought to him, but I know he gave to me the actual vision of higher range of human possibility, of severe and splendid triumph wrought in the power of divine grace.

These two incidents are taken from the early days and the latter days of the last twenty years, and they are typical of a countless succession of ministerial experiences which have poured wealth into my own treasury, enriching my possession of faith and hope and love. And this, too, will be the happy record of your own labours. While you give you will receive. While you comfort you will be comforted. While you counsel you will be enlightened. While you lift another's burden your own burden will be made light. For here, too, does the word of the Lord prevail: " He that findeth his life shall lose it: and he that loseth his life for My sake shall find it."

THE PREACHER AS A MAN OF AFFAIRS

"Like unto a merchantman"

———

L E C T U R E · S E V E N

THE PREACHER AS A MAN
OF AFFAIRS

" Like unto a merchantman "

IN the course of these lectures we have
considered the life and ministry of the
preacher in many varied relations,—in his
study, in his pulpit, and in the home, and
we have sought to realize, in all these
varying conditions, the line of purpose and
obligation. To-day we are to consider
quite another relation, not, perhaps, so
quick, and vital, and momentous as the
others, and yet one which seriously affects
the fruits of the others, either in the way
of retarding or advancing them. I am
to speak of the Preacher as a man of affairs, as one who meets and consults with
other men in the business management of
the church. And I am venturing to take
the direction and tone of my thought from
the teaching of the Master when He said
that " the kingdom of Heaven is like unto

a merchantman." That is to say, our Master commands, and appropriates, and sanctifies business instincts and aptitudes in the ministry of the kingdom. Talents and faculties, which are used in the affairs of the world, are to be used in the interests of our " Father's business." " The children of the world " are not to be wiser than " the children of light." We are not to " scrap " the business gifts, and rely upon some mysterious influence which works without them. We are to be vigilant, punctual, enterprising, decisive, surrendering all our senses to the work, and notably the king of all the senses, the sense which makes all other senses effective, the power of common sense. We are to be as merchantmen, men of sobriety, of wide sanity, of keen but cool judgment, alert but not hasty, zealous but circumspect, doing the King's business in a business-like way.

Now I think you would find it a very common confession that it is just here that many preachers fail. They may be accept-

able and even powerful in the pulpit.
They may be congenial and most welcome
in the home. But they are impossible in
business. No one can "get on" with
them. They have no sense of management or address. They are inopportune
when they think themselves seasonable,
they are stupid when they think themselves persistent. Their "goods" may be
admirable, but they lack the power to dis-
pose of them. They can hold their own
in the pulpit, but they have no strength
in the vestry. They can "carry" a congregation, they cannot lead the Diaconate
or the Session. They succeed as preachers
but they fail as merchantmen.

This lack of business ability may sometimes be traced to a deeper need from
which it directly springs, and I wish you
to consider two or three of these deeper
things upon which our real business aptitude depends. First of all then, I should
say that the primary requisite, if we are
to be successful men of affairs, is that we
ourselves be *men*. Some time ago an article

appeared in an American magazine entitled
" Is the preacher a molly-coddle? " In the
course of the article the writer makes the
following statement: " Among strong,
steadfast, manly business men, as well as
among the athletes of the baseball and foot-
ball field, there is a kind of belief or feeling
that all preachers belong in some measure
to the molly-coddle class." Now I suppose
a molly-coddle is a man who lacks resolu-
tion, energy, or hardihood, and that the
term is used in derision or contempt, and
I am afraid it expresses the conception of
the Christian preacher which is very commonly entertained by men of the world.
I know, of course, that the man of the
world is inclined to regard anything that
looks beyond his own material circle as
belonging to the effeminate, and his judgment is by no means the final standard
of strong and healthy life. And yet we
ought to listen to his judgment, and ponder its weight, even though we have finally
to discard it as practically worthless. If
there be any truth in the conception that

the preacher is lacking in the elements of true manliness we ought to see to it that the occasion of the judgment is changed. We must get more iron into our blood, more vision into our ideals, more vigour into our purposes, more sacrifice into our services, more tenacity into our wills. We must get rid of all that is soft, and lax, and flabby, and lethargic, and manifest to men that combination of strength and gentleness which is the fruit of the finest piety and the characteristic of all true manliness. On the side of vision the preacher's life should touch the romantic: on the side of labour he should touch the heroic: and in all his contact with men they should be made to feel his possession of a fresh and healthy vigour which clearly attests that he has found the fountain of vitality, and that he drinks of " the river of water of life." We certainly can never be successful merchantmen unless we are, first of all, men.

A second necessity, if we are to be competent men of affairs, is a competent knowledge of men. Our fellow-officers in the government of the Church are not like so many billiard-balls, devoid of individuality, having precisely the same weight, running in precisely the same manner, and by their inherent constitution determined by precisely the same initiatives to a common motion. When we are dealing with men the further we can get away from the conception of a billiard-ball the better it will be for the progress of our business. We must study men, we must know their differences as well as their unities, in order that we may know what are the different motives which will produce a common movement. You will be surprised how many types of character there are within the circle of a Session or a Diaconate. There are the facile men, swift in vision and in judgment, seeing their goal and leaping to decision. There are the slow-witted men, following the others like a carrier's wagon in the track of an automobile, arriving at clear vision through dim stages, first " seeing men as trees

walking," and troubled by doubts and in-
decisions. You will have these men to
deal with, and it is needful you should
know when they have only reached the
" tree-walking " stage, lest you should un-
wisely hurry them along the half-dark-
ened way. Then there are the genial men,
the men whose dispositions are confluent
and agreeable, a fervent fluid ready for
any mould. There are also the fixed, the
rigid, with dispositions that are only rarely
ductile, and who are hurt and resentful
if they are unseasonably squeezed into
some newly-fashioned mould. Most surely
you will meet such men, and it is a science
and art of the finest human perception and
ministry to soften their rigidity, almost
without their knowing it, and to conduct
their loosened spirit into the altered fashion of a new day. And there are the old
men, valuable because of their years, retro-
spective, often finding their " golden age "
in the days that are past, in " the days that
have been," their souls inclining to con-
servatism and venerable convention. And

there are the younger men, feeling "the days before them," thrilled by radiant vision, held by prospect rather than remembrance, inclined to take short cuts to desired ends, and to use very radical means to everything that obstructs their path. You may probably find all these singularly varied types within the fellowship of your church government, and they are your fellow-labourers in the business of the Church. Their co-operation is needed in the progress of the business, and you are the one who is to make the co-operation possible and effective. Some of your officers bring the equipment of eyes, while others bring the equipment of hands. Some again bring the wings of the fellowship while others can only supply feet. There is the artist and there is the artisan, the architect and the builder, the practical man and the dreamer of dreams. What are we going to do with all these unless we have some knowledge of men? Without that knowledge we may have intensity, but we shall lack leadership: we may have rashness, but we shall lack courage: there may be plenty "going on," but there will be little going forward: there may be even apparent progress, but there will also be restraint and reluctance which will chill the progress at its very heart.

How is this knowledge to be gained? It is to be gained chiefly by the general culture and refinement of our own character. Even the "communion of saints" must not be left to indolent chance, or to the discoveries of caprice. Fruitful communion is the reward of culture: fine correspondences among men are the rare issues of assiduous processes of moral discipline. We are not going to know men without "taking pains": which is only another way of saying that all valuable knowledge is reached at the end of a painful road. If we would know men we must discipline our powers of discernment. We must lift our eyes away from the self-circle, and turn them upon the factors moving in another man's circle. "Look not every man on his own things, but every man also on the things of others." That in itself is an exceedingly valuable exercise, just to recognize that there are other fields whose contour and features differ from our own. Then with disciplined discernments we must discipline our imagination. Common discernment may give us the external configuration of another man's field, but only a fine imagination will give us his interpretation of it. I am using the word "imagination" in the sense of enlightened sympathy, the power to get beneath another man's skin, and look out through his windows, and obtain his view of the world. I mean the power by which one man can identify himself with another, can become almost incorporate with another, and realize his general sense and appreciation of the things with which we deal. This is by no means easy: if any man thinks it easy, he has certainly not yet mastered the strong and gracious art. Casting my mind over biography and autobiography I do not know any man who possessed the gift in richer measure than Frederick Robertson of Brighton. He knew men in a most surprising manner, and, even though their judgments and convictions differed almost immeasurably from his own, he made laborious effort to understand their positions and to appreciate their sense and value. There is, consequently, a fine catholicity about his mind, and there is a noble comradeship about his manner, and he moves with an intelligent and sympathetic discernment of those whose conclusions he cannot share. But all this, I say, is not an easy attainment, it is a fruit of persistent culture: and if you and I are to be wise and strong leaders of men who are of very varying mental fashion and emotional moods, we must subject ourselves to the same quiet and serious discipline, and sympathetically and imaginatively appreciate their individuality, and realize their own peculiar points of view.

Now a discipline of this kind, the exercise of discernment and sympathetic imagination, will give us the invaluable possession of tact. I have sometimes heard it

said that if a man is devoid of tact by
nature he will never gain it as an acquisi-
tion: that it is always innate and never an
accomplishment. I don't believe it. I do
not attach so fatal and final a sovereignty
to the drift of heredity. I believe that
when God gives His good grace all good
graces are implicated in the gift, and that
by requisite care and culture they can be
evolved with all the order and certainty
of the production of flowers and fruits. I
believe that clumsy people can become
tactful, and that folk who are brusque and
abrupt can become gracious and courteous,
and that the indifferent and inconsiderate
can become thoughtful and sympathetic.
There is no excuse for our tactlessness, and
if even we are temperamentally tactless it
is our urgent duty to change it by the
ministries of discipline and grace.

But what trouble and disaster the want
of tact is working among the ministry of
the churches! I am appalled at times to
hear accounts of ministerial tactlessness
which are almost incredible in their exhibi-

tion of infantile ignorance of men. I have known many churches where spiritual life has been chilled, and spiritual enterprise has been ruined by the minister's tactless handling of men who were to carry his desires and purposes to fruition. Such ministers treat their fellow-officers as so many marionettes, and lo! the marionettes prove to be alive, with very marked and vivacious personalities, and there is consequent discord and strife. And therefore do I urge you to study and know your men: know them through the ministry of a hallowed and sympathetic imagination, and always bear them in strong and considerate regard. And you will come to possess tact, that fineness of feeling which can diagnose without touching, that mystical divining-rod which apprehends the hidden waters in the shyest and most secluded life. But even this is not enough. If our equipment for the knowledge of men is to be even passably complete we must exercise a genial sense of humour, by whose kindly light we shall be saved from pious stupidities, and from that grotesqueness of judgment which sees tragedy in comedy, griffins in asses, and mountains in mole-hills. Gentlemen, we need to know men, and when our men know that we know them, and respect and revere them, you may depend upon it we have got the key into the lock which will open their most secret gate.

I have one further word to say respecting our relations with those with whom we have to co-operate in managing the business of the Church. See to it that you exalt the great and noble dignity of their office. Hedge it about with reverence and prayerful regard. Let every man feel that no greater honour will ever come his way than his appointment to service in the Church of the Lord. Save the office from degenerating into a merely social distinction. Lift it up into a solemn and holy privilege in the Lord. Never let any man assume an office without the opportunity of gazing at his "high calling of God in Christ Jesus." Lift his eyes up to

the hills! Speak to him about it. Write
to him about it. And when he has entered
upon the office, and has even spent some
years in the service, seek his intimacy from
time to time that you may refresh his
sense of the sacred honour and responsibility of his vocation. You will find he
will welcome it, he will be grateful for it,
he will rise to it. And never allow any
countenance to be given to the divorce of
the secular and spiritual affairs of the
church, as though he who is working in
the administration of the temporalities is
engaged in a less sacred mission than he
who labours in the business of worship and
communion. Exalt them both alike; set a
common seal of sanctity upon them: and let
the " door-keeper in the house of our God "
feel that his office is as sacred as the office
of him who lights the candles at the altar,
or of him who bears the intercession into
the holy place. And remember this: the
atmosphere and spirit in which all business is done determines the real quality
and value of the business. And remem-

ber further: in a company of church officers it is the minister who is supremely
the creator of atmosphere, and that if he
is small, and churlish, and impatient, and
irritable, and self-willed, he makes conditions in which all sorts of petty things
breed and flourish: but if he is large, and
liberal, and patient, and self-controlled, he
creates a genial air and temper in which
all big things breathe easily, and generous
purposes find congenial hospitality and
support.

And now I want to offer you a few general principles of business management
which I think you will do well to heed in
your ministry. And the first is this:
Never move with small majorities. Never
take an important step in church life if a
large minority is opposed to your proposals. I inherited this principle from Dr.
Dale, and I have steadily honoured it all
through the years of my ministry. When
Dr. Dale's diaconate had discussed some
new proposals, and it was then found that
a minority of the deacons were opposed to

their adoption, the proposals were tabled,
and no action was taken. You may ex-
claim about the waste of time, the frequent and irritating delays! Yes, but remember that when Dr. Dale's diaconate
did move it moved to some purpose, with
unbroken solidity and with no hampering
hesitancy in its ranks. There was no half-
movement,—the feet advancing, but the
eyes held in lingering retrospect. It was
movement enlightened, expectant, and ir-
resistible. A small, lukewarm, unconvinced minority can chill the heart of even
a fine crusade. For you know how it is
with men. When men have been simply
"voted down," and carried forward against
their judgments, there often begins a
process of self-justification which greedily
seeks evidence to confirm their position.
"He, being willing to justify himself!"
That subtle quest governs our conduct
even more than we realize. We love to
maintain our own conclusions even when
some opposing action has been taken, and
we have more than a secret delight when

something happens which spoils the action, or in any way interferes with expected results. We do not realize that perhaps one cause of the sluggish or disappointing movement is just our own moody and suspicious reluctance. We think we are only spectators, watching others act, when in reality we are very busy actors, who being " willing " and eager " to justify " ourselves, are hampering those who began a movement which was opposed to our judgments. And so do I counsel you not to move with small majorities. Far better wait than try to run some new engine with lukewarm water. Wait for more enthusiasm: wait and pray for the unanimity of strong devotion. It is pre-eminently true in matters of church business that there must be light before there can be heat, there must be conviction before there can be resolute consecration, there must be an enlightened judgment before there can be a really vigorous and fruitful will. I have known churches ruined by the neglect of this principle. Great action has

been taken without serious union, and
premature movement has left behind an
unconvinced and irritated remnant, who
would not march as allies, and whose position scarcely gave them the helpful spirit
of friends. Perhaps in all these matters
we cannot do better than take for our
ideal the condition portrayed in a hidden
and little known passage in the Book of
Chronicles, where a strong and victorious
army is described as going " forth to battle, expert in war, fifty thousand, which
would keep rank: they were not of double
heart." I always think that a minister,
moving with a solidly united and sympathetic Diaconate or Session, can do almost anything!

The second principle of business management which I will offer you is this:
*avoid the notoriety and the impotence of
always wanting something new.* There
are some men who have new schemes for
their officers almost every time they meet.
Scheme after scheme is designed and pro-
duced, each new one effacing the signifi-

cance of the last, until in the multitude
of designs nothing is accomplished. The
officers are continually spending their time,
not in the inspiration of vision and task,
but in the soporific exercise of dreaming
dreams. I sometimes think it would be a
useful thing, at any rate it would be a
surprising and perhaps a humbling thing,
if a strong, vigilant committee could be
occasionally appointed to make a thorough
examination of the church minute-book for
the purpose of exhuming all resolutions
that were still-born, and all that had in-
dependent life but were never given a fair
chance of growing up, and all that by some
ill-chance were forgotten and had died
from sheer starvation and neglect. The
report of such a committee would provide
matter for a most important and significant meeting! It might be held once
every five years, or even more frequently
where the death-rate is abnormally high,
where schemes and purposes die almost as
soon as they are born. It might be called
a meeting for the disinterring and exami-

nation of resolutions which have never been carried out, proposals that never fructified, promising schemes which have drooped and no one knew the hour of their burial! It would be a very sombre and melancholy meeting. It would be like spending an hour in a graveyard. But I am sure the experience would not be without profit, and we might discover the folly of continually originating schemes merely to bury them, and of multiplying a family of plans and devices which immediately sink into their graves.

If we are competent merchantmen in the business of the Church we shall limit our schemes, and we shall operate them to the last ounce of our strength. We shall not waste and squander our power in twenty scouting excursions, but we shall use it in sinking one or two good mines, and working them with noble and persistent exploration. That is what we want in the ministry, men who will concentrate upon one or two promising mines, and week after week produce the invaluable ore. If

the pulpit is your mine, don't play with
it, work it night and day. If the Sunday-
School is your mine, sink your shaft deeper
and deeper, open out new seams and veins
of treasure, and let the mine abundantly
justify itself by its products. Whatever
may be your mine, put your strength into
it. I am a strong believer in a very few
schemes, but tried to the utmost; I believe
in a very few mines, but worked for all
they are worth. The life of our day
tempts us to diffuseness. We are tempted
to have too many irons in the fire, and we
don't beat any one of them to final
" shape and use." Gentlemen, have a
few well-designed and well-proportioned
schemes. Don't lose yourself in dreams.
Lay your hands upon a few things, and
hold on to them like grim death, and make
them pay daily tribute to the Lord your
God. Master something. Finish something, or be still working away at it when
the Lord promotes you to higher service.
That was the Master's way. " I have
finished the work which Thou gavest Me to

do." He "set His face" steadfastly to it, nothing drew Him aside, and He finished it. "Having loved His own which were in the world He loved them unto the end." His purposeful affection continued its ministry with tenacious and deathless persistency, and it never let go! And this, too, was the way of the Apostle Paul. "This one thing I do!" His life and work were controlled by a glorious concentration, and he held on to his track like a hound that has found the trail. Follow his inspired example. Don't be forever itching after novelties. Don't be continually shifting your ground. "Hold fast that which thou hast:" hold on to it, and "let patience have her perfect work."

I will offer you a third principle for your guidance in the business affairs of the Church. *Never mistake the multiplication of organization for the enlargement and enrichment of service.* Do not be deceived into thinking that you are doing work when you are only preparing to do it. It is very possible to elaborate our machinery and not increase our products. We may have much mechanism but little or no life. That is one of the immense perils of our day, and the ministers of the Church of Christ are peculiarly exposed to it. We organize, and organize, and organize! I suppose there was never a time when organization was so rife as it is to-day. You can hear the "noise" of the bones coming together. You can hear the "shaking" of their approach. Never was there such skill shown in the work of incorporation. Bone is fitted to bone, and the strength of sinews is added, and the grace of flesh and skin. But here is the vital question: is it only clever manufacture or is it inspired creation? Is it only a lovely corpse, or does it live—live, I mean, with the life of God? Much of it, I know, thrills with holy and effective life, and in its gracious movement it is possessed by breath divine. And yet how very much of our organization is only an articulated corpse! It does not carry a burden: it is rather a burden that has to be borne. It is an organization but not an organism! It has no central soul, no life, no breath. It stops short of the vital, the inspirational, the divine. It has got everything but God!

I believe that what the old world needs just now is not so much the multiplication of organization as the baptism of the Holy Ghost. We have piles of organization, but they lie prone upon the earth, incorporated death. We have got organization enough to revolutionize the race. It is not more schemes we want, more associations, more meetings: we want the breath and fire of the Holy Ghost. A small organization, with breath in it, can do the work of an army. I am not decrying the institutional. The institutional is necessary: it is imperative: but I fear that in these days we ministers may be so keen on organizing that we rest contented when the body is articulated, even though it lies stretched and breathless on the ground. We may be so intent upon committees that we have no time for the upper room. We may be so " public " that we forget

" the secret place." We may be absorbed in devising machinery and careless about the power which is to make it go. That is our peril. I know it. I feel it. We may be busy organizing and yet have no organic life. And if we only enlarge our " plant," and multiply our machinery, we are apt to think we are extending the Kingdom of our Lord and Saviour Jesus Christ. " Be not deceived." Keep your eyes on essentials. " Pray without ceasing," vigilantly watch for " the fruits of the Spirit," and smother any satisfaction which does not honour your great Redeemer's name.

There is a fourth principle which you will do well to heed when, with your fellow-labourers, you are estimating the business of the Church. *Never become a victim to the standard of numbers.* In this holy business statistics cannot measure enterprise. A church-roll by no means defines the limits of a church's influence and ministry. " The Kingdom of God cometh not with observation." It may be

moving here and there like the faintest
breathing, like the almost imperceptible
stirring of the air at the dawn. It may
be here and there in the creation of vision
and dream, in the loosening of hidden fear,
in the healing of unknown sorrow, in deliverance from secret sin. I know the comfort and inspiration that come to a minister in the open confession of God's children, when that confession is simple, and
serious, and true. But I am not going to
limit my conception of the fruits of my
ministry to products like these. There
are many people who find their Lord who
never find me. There are many children
of despondency and depression who steal
into my services, and who steal out again
with the feeling that " the winter is past,"
and that " the time of the singing of birds
is come. ' But no news of their spring-
time gets into my journal, or finds a place
in the diaries of the Church. Many a weary
business-man, who for a whole week has
been the victim of the dusty plains, trails
into the church, and he gets a vision of the

glory of the hills of God, and his soul is restored, but no tidings of his soul's journeyings is given to me. Gentlemen, we should be astonished with a great surprise if we knew all the secret happenings which take place every time we minister of the Lord Jesus in sincerity and in truth! *Something always happens*—deep and gracious and beautiful, and the great Husbandman, who never overlooks or loses any fruit, will gather it unto everlasting life. So I counsel you not to be burdened by the menace of statistics, and do not permit your strength to be sapped by worries which you ought to quietly lay upon the love of God. "Trust in the Lord, and do good: so shalt thou dwell in the land, and verily thou shalt be fed."

And the last counsel which I will give you as merchantmen in the business of the Kingdom is this:—*you never help the business by advertising yourself.* Self-advertisement is deadly in the ministry of the Lord Jesus. Puffy, showy paragraphs concerning ourselves and our work: ego-

tistical recitals of our powers and attainments: all forms of self-obtrusion and self-
aggression: all these are absolutely fatal
to the really deepest work committed to
our hands. Our fellow-labourers know
when our work is marred by self-conceit.
The devil is delighted when he can lure us
into self-display. Our own highest powers
shrink and wither when we expose them to
the glare of self-seeking publicity. They
cannot bear a light like that, and they
speedily lose their strength and beauty. I
urge you to avoid it. Never tell people
what a clever fellow you are. Never write
a private paragraph to the newspaper giving its readers the same information. It
was said of the Master Whom we serve,
" He shall not strive, nor cry, neither shall
any man hear His voice in the streets."
" It was the way the Master went. Shall
not the servant tread it still? " Of one
thing we can be perfectly sure: when we
display ourselves we hide our Lord; when
we blow our own trumpet men will not
hear " the still small voice of God."

And now I have done. I have spoken to you in these lectures from the journals of my own life, the findings of my own experience. I thought you might like to know how one man has found the road into the service of which you are consecrating your life. I have told you where I have found perils, and where I have found arbours of rest and refreshing springs. Your road may be very different from mine, and yet I think the dominant features will be the same. You will have your Slough of Despond, your hill "Difficulty," your alluring Bye-path Meadow, your Valley of Humiliation, your Enchanted Ground where the spirit gets very drowsy, and your clear hill-tops with bewitching visions of Beulah Land, where the birds sing and the sun shines night and day. But you will surely find that, however swiftly changing may be the character of your road, your provision in Christ is most abundant.

My brethren, you are going forth into a big world to confront big things. There is " the pestilence that walketh in darkness," and there is "the destruction that wasteth at noonday." There is success and there is failure, and there is sin, and sorrow, and death. And of all pathetic plights surely the most pathetic is that of a minister moving about this grim field of varied necessity, professing to be a physician, but carrying in his wallet no balms, no cordials, no caustics to meet the clamant needs of men. But of all privileged callings surely the most privileged is that of a Greatheart pacing the highways of life, carrying with him all that is needed by fainting, bruised, and broken pilgrims, perfectly confident in Him "Whom He has believed." Brethren, your calling is very holy. Your work is very difficult. Your Saviour is very mighty. And the joy of the Lord will be your strength.